Praise for C[...]

M000205530

'After twenty years of working tog[...] have nothing but praise for Owen Fitzpatrick ... His new book fills a gap in the literature of the field of NLP and the subject of charismatic living. More importantly, it is an everyday guide to vigorously pursue the life you want in a way that shines.'

Dr Richard Bandler

'Charisma is the impression that you create in the mind of another person. Having spent time personally and professionally with Owen over the past few years, I know that the impression he creates in audiences around the world is one of a charismatic master of communication. *The Charismatic Edge* is a gem of a book. It has distilled years of knowledge and research into an essential 'how to' guide for anyone wishing to understand the secrets of being more charismatic. Owen Fitzpatrick's unique psychological insight makes this book the finest book on charisma I have read. It is concise, well-written, and goes to the heart and head of what charisma really is. I highly recommend it.'

Paul Boross, author of *The Pitch Doctor*

'The cross between the Sherlock Holmes, Gregory House and James Bond of the corporate arena: Owen sees things that no one else does, conveys it as straight as you can get and moves quietly in, tackling the problem with a steely grit and relentless determination that ensures the problem is, once and for all, eliminated.'

Joseph Higgins, Finance Manager

'As a business leader with over 20 years' experience, I have read countless books and academic papers on the subject of charisma and its importance to success. Owen Fitzpatrick's book, however, not only sets the benchmark in this regard, it also sets out clearly in layman's terms how anyone following his systematic approach can learn the skills necessary to excel in this field. He is fast becoming the 'go-to' guy for business leaders wishing to improve their charisma skills and I therefore have no hesitation whatsoever in recommending him and his book to you.'

Robert Orr, CEO

'Having coached some of the world's most recognisable actors and many dynamic corporate leaders, it's often hard to explain to people why some people are mesmeric and others simply are not. In this book Owen Fitzpatrick has broken the code and unlocked all the secrets to allow anyone to confidently brim with charismatic confidence. For anyone who has a message and wants to connect with others in the most meaningful way, *The Charismatic Edge* tells you how to authentically reach peak performance.'

Poll Moussoulides, International Voice Coach

About the Author

Owen Fitzpatrick is a psychologist and an expert on Charisma, NLP and High Performance. He has worked with billionaires and Olympic athletes and has taught tens of thousands of people in more than twenty countries how to communicate more powerfully and perform brilliantly. He is founder of the Online Charisma Training Academy and co-founder of the Irish Institute of NLP, co-author of three books with Dr Richard Bandler (co-founder of NLP). Owen has studied Strategic Negotiation in Harvard Business School, been coached by the media coach to Bill and Hillary Clinton and met Indian gurus and Hollywood celebrities in his quest to understand what the greatest communicators on earth do differently. Owen lives in Dublin. *www.owenfitzpatrick.com*

The Charismatic Edge

The Art of Captivating and Compelling
Communication

Owen Fitzpatrick

Gill & Macmillan

To the late Dr Elizabeth Dunne, for all you have taught me and for believing in me in university. It was a great honour learning from you. You are very much missed.

To Dr Richard Bandler, the most charismatic person I have ever met, for being an inspiration and a legend in bringing a set of skills to the world that has quite literally changed it. Thank you, Richard, for all you have taught me and all you have done for me. I am where I am thanks in no small degree to your support and help.

All NLP techniques are used with permission of Dr Richard Bandler.

Gill & Macmillan
Hume Avenue, Park West, Dublin 12
with associated companies throughout the world
www.gillmacmillanbooks.ie

© Owen Fitzpatrick 2013
978 07171 5608 5

Typography design by Make Communication
Print origination by O'K Graphic Design, Dublin
Printed in Sweden by ScandBook AB

This book is typeset in 10.5/13 pt Minion.

The paper used in this book comes from the wood pulp of managed forests. For every tree felled, at least one tree is planted, thereby renewing natural resources.

A CIP catalogue record for this book is available from the British Library.

5 4 3 2

Contents

Acknowledgements

In reality, this should be the biggest chapter of the book. The number of incredible people I have in my life is humbling, and the impact they have had on me is immeasurable.

A huge thank you first must go to all my family and friends, of course, who make me the kind of person I am today.

I'd like to say a big thank you to Fergal Tobin and the wonderful team at Gill & Macmillan especially Nicki Howard, Teresa Daly and D Rennison Kunz for their outstanding help. They provided fantastic support and were a real pleasure to work with.

Thanks to Marjorie and Brian Fitzpatrick, quite simply the greatest human beings on the planet. Words can't express how much you mean to me or how much you've done for me. I owe you so much and I love you even more.

Lucy Cullen and Aoife O'Reilly, my two god-daughters and the two most beautiful girls in the world. I love you very much. My uncle Shea, sister Emer, brother-in-law Robert and all my cousins and family, for your love, support and advice. I'm so lucky to have such an incredible family. My cousin Dónal Kearney, for his super support and outstanding work editing and helping me with the manuscript.

Sandra Pou Van Biezen, international director of marketing for Owen Fitzpatrick International, for reviewing the manuscript and giving me suggestions, not to mention being an incredible friend, support and colleague on the way to taking over the world.

Denise Da Costa for fantastic support and help with research for the book. I'm blessed to have you in my life.

My friend and co-trainer Brian Colbert, and Theresa Colbert, manager of the Irish Institute of NLP, for being loyal, supportive, fantastic friends and for all the great times.

John and Kathleen LaValle, for their wonderful support, advice and help. It's an honour to know you both, and I will never forget what you have done for me in helping me in my life.

Alessio Roberti, my friend and colleague, for believing in the charisma book from the very beginning.

My NLP colleagues and friends, such as Michael Connolly, Kate Benson, Yurina Shiraishi, Elena Martelli, Hugh Street, Miriam Birney, Rocio Suarez, Xavi Pirla, Maha Daoudi, Tom Ziglar, Margaret Considine, Dan Buriak, Jay Chopra, Sri Hari, Uwe and Maria, Stefano Manassera and Yeliz Ruzgar, and all my many promoters and friends around the world, for your support, encouragement and help.

To Dave Meier and Paddy O'Shea, two terrific professionals who help me reach the world.

Jim Rohn, Zig Ziglar, Paul McKenna, Joel Roberts, Michael Sheenan and Brendon Burchard, who all taught me valuable insights on charisma.

Poll Moussoulides, a partner along the way of the charisma journey, as well as the entire Charisma Bootcamp team . . . Karl Spain, Kev Fitzsimmons, Terry Harmer, Sonya Lennon, Paul Boross, Noel Davidson, Paula Mullin and Leopi, and the great help from Lorna Sixsmith, Breandán Kearney, Steve Fahy, Ornella, John O'Connell and Cormac Moore. Also, Anna Aparicio, for doing an outstanding job as co-ordinator for both Charisma Bootcamps.

D. P. Fitzgerald, for your fantastic help with everything. You, sir, are a legend and super friend.

TGRO and Michelle Orr, for all your wonderful advice, support and friendship. You inspire me on a regular basis.

And my friends Eddie Collins, Dave O'Reilly, Shane Lynch, Joe Higgins, Ruairi Curran, Ruairí O'Connor, Cristina Granizo, Gillian McNamara Fowley, Lauren Inkster, Liz O'Reilly, Siobhan McCarthy, Ruth Collins, Steve Zhik, Valerie Solodukho, Raquel Nayberg, Tamir Elghanayan, Brian Fowley, Tomas a.k.a. Spartacus, Philipe Joly, Anahi Alvarez Anta, Rachel Joseph, Karl Rooney, Paul Kiernan, Marie Curran, John Reynolds, Sabrina Hussain, Oui and Niels, Simon Dowd, Erin McCann, Lynda Morrissey, Lorraine Higgins, Richard Collins, Alan Curran, Mark Bagnall, Niall Boylan, Jennifer Lynch, Alberto Simone, Anca Irina Lefter, Cindy Reid, Gail Ramsay Ratcliffe, Alina and Andreea Serbann, Jason Wilson, Olivia Lavelle, Ben Carrigan and Maurice Whelan, and many more for being a wonderful support for me. Also, for the help in RTÉ, my friends John, Teresa, June, Alan, Kieran and Cormac.

Chapter 1

Introduction

You can be more

Some people are intimidated when talking to large numbers of people in an entertaining way. Not me.

DAVID BRENT

Imagine you wake up one morning at your very best. You get up feeling great, full of energy and motivated for the day ahead. You brush your teeth and have a shower and run through the day you're about to have. And you know you can handle it. You know it's going to go well.

Imagine every interaction goes as well as it could possibly go. You feel extremely confident and sure of yourself yet humble and interested in others. You are at your most engaging, entertaining and persuasive. You can read other people effortlessly and know exactly what to say. You get through to whoever you speak to easily and motivate them, inspire them, connect with them.

Imagine you're clear and compelling in how you relate to others, while remaining caring and compassionate. You use the right word at the right time in the right situation with the right person, each and every time. You handle difficult conversations brilliantly and you're an obvious leader. You're the life and soul of the party and you embrace challenges with a smile and a sense of knowing that, come what may, 'everything's gonna be alright.'

If this were true, what would life be like for you? What would your personal experiences be like? What would your professional life be like? How would people see you? How would you see yourself? How would they feel about you? How would you feel about yourself? My guess is that, if you're like me, the thought of what this would be like really excites you.

I've spent the last twenty years studying and practising everything and anything I could find to do with communication and influence, leadership and charisma. Like you, I have an interest in—a passion for—what makes people tick and how to perform at your absolute best. If we could only be at our very best it would transform our world. It would have a huge impact on our income, our interactions, our inner sense of happiness. We know this. And yet we rarely live up to our best. We rarely reach our potential. Why is this? I believe there are two core reasons: we don't know how to, and we're scared to.

THE DEATH OF PERSONALITY

The reality is that the vast majority of people on this planet are not living up to the very best versions of themselves. Many people don't come across as even remotely interesting or engaging. Instead, their personalities are on life support, only awakening on special occasions within the comfort zones of close friends and family. They're not experiencing enough of what life can be like, they're simply surviving. Their heart is beating, but it's not feeling.

Sit on a bus or train and you will see little evidence of life. Facial expressions rarely change, and people avoid eye contact, hoping they won't have to converse with each other. Despite such close proximity, we have never felt so far apart from our fellow-humans.

We hide who we are when we meet people, in our social life, in business. We try to be who we think we should, dress how we think we should and speak how we think we should. We do so to fit in. We want others to approve of us, to love us, to be impressed by us. We crave acceptance.

When asked about why we aren't very sociable we dig deep within our creativity for a plausible excuse. We explain that we're shy even though we might really want to be confident. We explain that we're happy as we are and are just 'this' type of person or 'that' type of person. But we're lying to ourselves. We're lying because we are scared.

Of course, there's nothing wrong with having a preference for being introverted. But using that as an excuse not to communicate as best we can is where we make the biggest mistake. Some of the most successful people in the world are introverted, but when they need to communicate they can. Barack Obama is an example of this. One of the most charismatic politicians of our time, Obama is reported as being an introvert, yet he is able to communicate with impact when it's required of him.

The excuses we tell ourselves permit us to justify a lack of effort, or a dearth of results. And the fascinating thing is this: the most obvious difference between very successful people and everyone else is that the successful make far fewer excuses.

However, many of us are afraid of contact—fearful of interaction, terrified of making a fool of ourselves. We're petrified of what others think of us. This stifles us, traps us, limits us. The result of this is that we live an average life, in average circumstances, and we get by.

Let me ask you a question. Is 'getting by' enough for you? I ask you because it was never enough for me. I've always wanted more. In order to get more I learnt that two things need to happen. Firstly, you need to get over the fears that prevent you from doing so. Then you need to know what to do to impact others more.

To get over the fears that hold you back you need to look inward and examine who you are—who you really are. You need to get to know your character—the truth about yourself. You need to get to like yourself and be comfortable with being yourself much more frequently. Then you will be able to overcome fear. You will be authentically 'you'.

Once you reach that milestone the next step will be learning what to do to become more effective at delivering your message. And the rules have changed. The social and corporate worlds today are radically different from those of the past. Knowing how to be at your best in communicating is a whole new game at the present day.

THE NEW RULES OF COMMUNICATION IN THE TWENTY-FIRST CENTURY

Globalisation has meant that our friendships are often dispersed around the world. The internet has created a new kind of virtual friendship that emphasises shortened bursts of written communication. We tweet and post Facebook photos, always planting a smile on our face as we try to get others to see us in a positive light.

We're now friends who market to each other. We advertise how we are, what we think and how we feel in spurts of revelation by means of social media. We communicate through text messages and email in a virtual world, a virtual reality. And when we do interact in the real (physical) world, things have changed.

We no longer live in a world where we are granted full attention. Now we have to earn it. We have to grab it. We have to keep it. We face competition, not just in the business world but in our personal lives. There are so many other things someone can be doing, so many other choices they have instead of spending time with us, that we have to be of constant interest and relevance to them.

In this world of limited attention you have to understand what to do in order to stand out, engage and influence others. That means learning from the thousands of years of study and research in the field of communication into how you can do so with impact. It means learning all you can about the psychology of influence, personal development, neuro-linguistic programming, leadership, marketing, sales, comedy, storytelling and media training, to name but a few areas of study.

You have to be prepared to practise skills that have been tried and tested in the modern world, to duplicate the strategies used by the most compelling and charismatic speakers and to apply the principles and insights of the very best leaders, salespeople, politicians, lawyers, preachers, actors, voice coaches, screenwriters, therapists, life and business coaches, trainers, speakers, novelists, socialites, attraction experts and marketing geniuses.

The beauty is that, regardless of their field, all these experts offer us powerful insights into what makes some people engaging and compelling to listen to and others not. The Holy Grail we're discussing here is the discovery of the things you need to know and do to make the most impact.

The wonderful news is that we have never known more about how the mind works than we do today. Brain research has taught us more about the mind in the last three years than in the last three thousand. We have never known more about how people are influenced. We have never known more about how people make decisions and about how to keep them focused. The information is there.

If only there was a way to comb through the terabytes of information and find the most important principles and insights that relate to creating a powerful effect when you communicate. If only this could be packed into a book you could read in a matter of hours.

That is my goal in this book. In it, I will share almost twenty years of experience and the most prevalent insights into human communication to answer two crucial questions: how you can become the very best version of yourself, and how you can express yourself to others in an engaging and memorable way.

So, my purpose is twofold: to help you become more *you* and to help you express yourself to others in such a way that *they want* more of *you*. When you accomplish this you will have what I call the 'charismatic edge'.

WHAT'S IN THIS BOOK?

You'll find it split into four parts. The first is called 'Step up: The attitude of charisma'. Here I will invite you to explore *you*—the real you—and share with you strategies and techniques that will enable you to be more like you, and to like you more. This tackles the ever-pressing issue of becoming far more secure in yourself.

The second part is 'Step forward: The actions of charisma'. Here I will share with you the very best insights and skills for understanding how to put yourself across to others in the most desirable manner, and for maximising your physicality, body language and voice.

In the third part, 'Stand out: The art of charisma', you will learn the four key skills for being an effective communicator and how to influence people, make people laugh, tell captivating stories and speak with impact in public.

The final part, 'Stand for: Applications of charisma', will explain how to apply the insights you've gained to a number of areas, to help you present the best version of yourself to the world. This will include leadership, sales, interviews, flirting, relationships, parenting and lots more.

Whatever area of business you're in, or whatever aspect of your life you'd like to make more of an impact in, what you learn in this book will have massive consequences for you, both in your personal life and in your professional life. When you apply the ideas herein, life will never be the same again for you. But not only for you. I believe that what this world needs more than ever is a revolution in how we relate to each other. It needs more people to stand up and be themselves.

I want this book to help both yourself and others. I hope you can share the ideas I present to you with your friends and colleagues, because I believe we need a change, a shift, a new viewpoint on ourselves and on the world. I hope you will join with me in this. I want to challenge you not just to be your best, but to do your best.

This book is not designed to swamp you with the vast amount of existing research. I've provided a reference to some that you can follow up on, but for many of the insights I present I've avoided footnotes, expansive references, jargon and technical terms. I've done the legwork on this one over the past few years and filled my brain with studies and theories, facts and opinions. Here you get the nutrients—without the fat!

WHY LISTEN TO ME?

So, what makes me worth reading, then? What makes me the expert? Let me answer these questions in the next few paragraphs so that I don't have to keep 'subtly' telling you why I'm great for the rest of the book (drives me crazy when I see that!) and can instead put all my focus on the most important person: you.

As a psychologist, I've worked with tens of thousands of people individually and in courses, teaching and training many aspects of personal and professional development, charisma perhaps most of all. I've coached billionaires and Olympic athletes to perform at their best. I've worked with CEOs on presenting themselves better on stage and in the media. I've trained trainers and teachers to become better public speakers. I've travelled to more than seventy-five countries, and I've taught people in more than twenty to become more effective in how they communicate with others.

I presented my own prime-time show on RTÉ for two years and have been interviewed by the leading television and radio interviewers in Ireland. I'm the founder of the Charisma Bootcamp, a multi-speaker event for which I invited twelve speakers to Dublin—including a top voice coach, stylist, magician, comedian, pitch doctor and authority on leadership—to teach various aspects of communication. I've taught my charisma courses and ideas all over the world, including in Japan, Thailand, India, Italy, Spain and Colombia.

Having read thousands of books on psychology and communication, I did my Master's thesis in applied psychology on 'Gurus and Charisma'. I'm a qualified psychotherapist and hypnotherapist and a licensed master trainer of neuro-linguistic programming. I've been mentored by, and written a number of books with, the joint creator of NLP, Richard Bandler (teacher of Paul McKenna and Anthony Robbins).

I've studied media skills with one of the best media trainers in the world, Joel Roberts, and have been personally coached by Michael Sheehan, media adviser to Bill and Hillary Clinton. I studied strategic negotiation at Harvard Business School and deliver leadership-development courses and training on innovation, communication, time management, influence and motivation, as well as delivering keynote speeches for multinational companies and world-class market leaders.

Now, at this point I could either go on or I could say this: I don't tell you all this to impress you but to 'impress upon you' something. But the reality is that I do want to impress you. I do want you to be impressed—very impressed. I'm impressed. But why? Very simply, because it wasn't always like that for me.

Today I work in a job I thoroughly enjoy and I have a life I'm really happy with. But my story doesn't begin here.

WHY DO I CARE?

The real reason you should listen to me is because of my story. It's not just that I want to share my story with you: I need to. Why? Because I believe that the people I've listened to in life, the people who got through to me, have done so only when I felt they cared and when I felt I understood why they did. So let me explain why I care—a lot—about you getting what you want from this book.

I don't come from a broken home. I wasn't abused by anyone. I haven't suffered through terrible grief or tragedy. But twenty years ago I wanted to die. Not only did I want to die, each day when I came home from school I'd plot my downfall, write suicide letter after suicide letter and try to summon up the courage to end it all.

Hiding away from the world, I used to go to my room and scratch my wrists every day with a compass. This continued for a while, and my reasons were all connected with my experience at school. I had no real friends. I was seen as a reject, an outcast, a loser. I was the opposite to popular. I struggled every day in school, hating myself, hating my life. I felt like I had been born destined to always be alone, always be rejected. To me there was no hope. I was trapped inside my body, my personality, and I was left without anything to look forward to.

The pain I experienced eventually drove me to do something: it drove me to start studying. Not schoolwork but everything I could get my hands on about popularity. I became fascinated with reading books on self-improvement, and I focused on learning all I could about becoming better with other people. I was tenacious and studied as if my life depended on it.

Because it did.

Over the next few years in finishing school and university, I studied part time to become a therapist and NLP trainer. This is basically a system where you learn how to change the way you think, feel and communicate. In university, I studied human development and psychology and after eight years walked away with a Master's degree in applied psychology and a thesis on charisma.

The whole time, I was obsessed—obsessed with understanding the secrets of the most powerful speakers, salespeople, trainers, seducers, celebrities, politicians, leaders; obsessed with understanding how I could start getting similar results; obsessed with understanding if I could truly change my life. It wasn't just an academic obsession: it was a live-saving obsession. Bit by bit, I applied what I learnt. Bit by bit, I began to be myself more. Bit by bit, I stood out, engaged others and became more persuasive.

I learnt what worked and what didn't, what helped and what didn't, what could change and what couldn't. I found out what the most successful negotiators do in billion-dollar deals and how best-selling authors prepare for 'Oprah'. I understood how Hollywood screenwriters create the most charismatic characters. I discovered how the best preachers and speakers fire up their audience and how top comedians time their delivery to have their audiences dying with laughter.

What I didn't expect was that the secrets I sought were not to be found in some communication strategy, but in the hearts of the people I studied. They were in the character of the inspirational individuals. I soon travelled the world teaching what I'd learnt to tens of thousands of people. And I kept refining what I learnt, adapting it as the world changed and was transformed.

So, what I share with you here is purely the result of a lot of hard work. It is the result of a lot of trial and error. It is the result of a burning obsession that has led me to understand this topic so well. The book you are about to read packs in the most essential principles I have ever learnt, the same principles for which people have attended my courses over the last twenty years and that have cost me tens of thousands of euros to learn. So, drink deep the wisdom in these pages, for herein lie insights that can help you transform your world.

THE EDGE OF CHARISMA

Before I discuss what I mean by 'edge' let me just explain what I mean by 'charisma'. It is an impression of yourself that you create in the mind of another person. It may be one of you as funny or inspiring, entertaining or fascinating, persuasive or powerful; but whatever it is it engages them in some way. They listen to you, watch you and want to know more.

By edge I mean having that 'something extra', the quality that marks you out from the average and keeps you a step ahead of the game. This something extra is the knowledge of what to do to stand out, engage others and persuade them. Having that skill in the current economic environment is absolutely critical. It's a skill you can't afford not to learn. Most people never learn this skill for one reason: they were lied to.

YOU'VE BEEN LIED TO

Imagine you were in a room with the following people: John F. Kennedy, Adolf Hitler, Marilyn Monroe, Oprah Winfrey, Barack Obama, Madonna, Steve Jobs, Michael Jackson, Mahatma Gandhi, Lady Gaga, Bill Clinton, Aung San Suu Kyi, Lenny Kravitz, George Clooney, Robert Downey, Jr, Eleanor Roosevelt, the Dalai Lama, Frank Sinatra, Kim Il Sung and Martin Luther King, Jr. Or, here in Ireland, imagine you were in a room with Charles Haughey, Mary McAleese, James Joyce, Gerry Ryan, Miriam O'Callaghan, Michael Collins, Mary Robinson, Oscar Wilde, Ryan Tubridy, Maeve Binchy, Bono, Marian Finucane and Gay Byrne.

Who would you go to? Who is the first person you'd want to talk to (or punch)? One thing is certain: for each of you reading this, I'm very sure I'd get different responses. We have different preferences and different perceptions of what it means to be charismatic. Here's the problem, though: we've been lied to. We've been lied to because we've been told that charisma is impossible to attain and that it's possessed by these larger-than-life characters because of their genes or childhood environment. The reality is quite different. So let me now, quickly and decisively, eliminate the three predominant myths that surround the idea of charisma.

Myth no. 1: Charisma is a personality trait

The main theory that caught on about charisma is that it's some sort of trait or quality that some people have and others haven't. According to this theory, what comprises 'being charismatic' is the possession of good looks, energy, confidence and enthusiasm, along with the quality of a person's eyes and the quality of their voice.

This makes sense from the point of view of how we describe people and charisma: 'He is a charismatic person,' 'She has charisma.' However, there are plenty of examples of people who don't possess qualities such as these. You think Hitler was sexy? That's my point. (By the way, if you do, you've got issues.)

I have one simple argument that instantly disables this notion: babies.

I have got the two most beautiful god-daughters on the planet. Both of them light me up with a smile whenever I see them. Whenever I'm with them I barely notice anyone else. You may be aware that when you walk into a room and see a baby or toddler they will always capture your attention. They will immediately command your focus. Also, you really want a baby to like you. For some reason it's really important. Babies and toddlers are naturally charismatic. We find ourselves drawn to them and want to be around them. We don't know what they're going to do next, and they know how to get through to others.

Myth no. 2: Charisma is just a set of behaviours

There are many books that argue that charisma is just a set of behaviours, that people are construed as charismatic because of what they do, the way they present themselves in terms of how they look, sound and communicate with others. The idea is that you can train someone to be charismatic by having them dress differently, walk differently or speak differently.

Although it certainly enables the person on one level, this theory falls down for the following reason: how you feel about yourself internally will come across to others no matter what you learn to do with your body language or voice. People get a feeling around you, and that feeling is based not only on how you communicate to them but also on the kind of person you are.

The way you think affects how you come across to others. The state you're in and the beliefs that guide your behaviour are critical factors in developing charisma.

Myth no. 3: You can't change—just accept your limitations

Some people will argue that charisma and other 'Western' concepts are overrated and that we must simply accept what is, rather than search for the solution all the time. They will suggest that we must just stay in the present and observe our surroundings and avoid attempting to 'achieve' all the time. To a certain extent they're correct about the overarching need many people seem to have to attain their goals. But I wish to make a different point in this book.

This is not about 'achieving' a life full of friends, adoration and popularity. I want to go much deeper than that. I want you to find the character within and accept yourself more deeply than you ever have, because it's from that place that you will recognise that charisma has a lot to do with being in the present. It has a lot to do with presence. For it's in letting yourself become absorbed in your experiences that you fully engage with others. However, in order to do this we need something deeper than a few skills or strategies.

You see, we all think we know what charisma means, who is charismatic and who isn't. Most of us would agree on those mentioned above—all very different people, and yet they could all be deemed charismatic. We know charismatic individuals are preachers and great leaders, evil dictators and promoters of cults. Their one common characteristic is that they've all made an impact on the world. This wasn't a result of some 'trick' or 'technique'; it wasn't simply about some 'skill' or 'strategy'. It was because of who they were, deep down. They were powerful characters—not necessarily all good, but powerful.

Stephen Covey, in his classic book *The 7 Habits of Highly Effective People*, suggested that if we want to bring about an effective change we need to think in terms of the 'character ethic' rather than the 'personality ethic'. We need to think of the great qualities we can unlock in ourselves rather than the superficial practices that can boost our popularity in the short term.

I want to propose a radically different way of thinking about charisma. I see charisma as being far deeper than most people suppose. I see it as consisting of three dimensions. I believe that it's rooted firmly on the inside, in the attitude and character, practised on the outside through our actions and behaviours, and, finally, developed in our interactions through abilities and skills.

THREE-DIMENSIONAL CHARISMA

I believe that we all have charismatic potential. I know this because I've seen people become charismatic, and if it's possible for them it's possible for anyone. In studying the elements that constitute charisma, I've discovered that the qualities of charisma are all things that can be worked on and improved on. It requires effort, but the results make it worthwhile.

Through my analysis of charisma, I found that the qualities of charismatic people are three-dimensional.

1. Charismatic attitudes: This includes the beliefs that charismatic individuals have about themselves and about their interaction with the world. It also includes what I call 'charismatic states', which are the internal states that individuals experience when they're at their most charismatic.

2. Charismatic actions: This refers to the way in which individuals present themselves through their body language, voice and non-verbal gestures, and even how they dress.

3. Charismatic abilities: Here we're talking about the skills that individuals use to construct themselves as charismatic, such as the ability to use humour well, the art of persuasion and the craft of storytelling or public speaking.

You can work on these three qualities. The key is to begin by getting your beliefs right and then to develop the states, behaviours and skills necessary to reach a charismatic state. These qualities will be improved by following the suggestions and guidelines I present. The next step is to decide where and how you're going to apply this learning. So you will also get a chance to discover how you can use what you will be absorbing in a multitude of situations.

To sum up, here is my definition and model of charisma: the art of creating an impression of yourself in the mind of another person as someone who is interesting, entertaining, captivating, compelling or convincing.

Three-dimensional charisma is the model of developing powerful, personal charisma. It exists in three dimensions: your attitude, your actions and your abilities. When you work on all three levels you develop a far more powerful presence and a charisma that lasts.

This book is not just a guide for what specifically you can do to transform how you impact the world. It's something that will challenge you, provoke you and reveal to you the most fascinating insights we have gained over the last hundred years into ourselves and how we interact with each other. Your conversations will never be the same again, for you will understand more of what's going on, and you will understand—in times when you most need to win over the hearts and minds of others—what to say, how to say it, even why to say it. The book you hold in your hands is a master-class in the field of human communication. This master-class can help you build a more charismatic brain. How is this possible? Surely our brains can't learn to become more charismatic. Well, they can, and here's why.

BORN TO BE WILD: GENES, NEUROLOGY AND CHARISMA

When I was in university we'd be asked every other day to write about whether some psychological trait was a result of our genes or our environment. The nature-nurture debate is one that still torments students of psychology throughout the world. And, if I may be so bold, it's a really stupid waste of time to try and answer that question. For almost any psychological trait you mention I will give you the same answer: it's both. And, often, it isn't even that relevant what the exact percentages are. In most cases they seem to be around the fifty-fifty mark. What I believe is useful is to understand to what degree we have control over such traits. What I believe is even more useful is to understand how we can actually affect them ourselves.

You see, the nature-nurture debate had a missing piece: it didn't account for our ability to deliberately affect a trait. It presupposed that the way we were nurtured or the way our environment shaped us was the only way that a non-genetic influence could affect how we behave. The reality, however, is that more and more we're learning that we have the ability to alter our brains and even, some exciting new research suggests, our genes.

There are billions of brain cells or neurons in our brain. Between them there are nerve connections or bridges that connect to each other. When you learn something for the first time, your brain creates a new bridge (also called a synaptic connection) between neurons, and the more you practise it, the more you reinforce that connection so that it becomes permanent.

If you take control over the way you think and feel you effectually take control over the way your brain functions. Even if you're genetically predisposed to being anxious or depressed you have the ability to rewire your neurology by training your mind to make the kind of connections that produce confidence and calmness. Meditation, hypnosis, NLP, and mindfulness have all been shown to be very powerful ways of building a better brain.

Your brain releases chemicals that affect your feelings all the time. The fact that you have a say in this is incredible news. And it's news that can change your life. For if you change your thinking you will change your neurochemistry. Your brain will release more dopamine, serotonin and endorphins (feel-good chemicals). It will release less cortisol and neuro-inhibitors (stress chemicals). You will think more clearly and communicate more powerfully.

So to the question 'Is it possible to build a more charismatic brain?' the answer, I believe with absolute certainty, is a resounding *Yes*. Our brains can be rewired to make us more confident and better communicators, and our true potential hasn't even begun to be fully explored.

The book you're reading contains many exercises. If you do them you will be starting the process of rewiring how your brain connects and ensuring that you start to feel happier with yourself, more confident, more relaxed and more inspired by the opportunity to make an impact.

To make your brain more charismatic you will be making a number of attitude, physiological, behavioural and emotional shifts. Also, the brain learns by repetition, so it's not good enough to do something just once or twice: the key is to make it a habit. Habits operate on a particular neural pathway. When you repeatedly go down this pathway you increase its efficiency and go down it quicker, and the habit becomes more and more automatic.

This is connected with the four stages of learning. The first stage is the unconscious incompetence phase. This is when you don't know that you can't do something: your inability is not even in your consciousness. The next stage is the conscious incompetence phase, when you're aware that you can't do something. The third stage is the conscious competence phase. This is when you can do something when you give all your concentration and attention to it. Finally, the fourth stage is when you practise enough to develop unconscious competence. That means you can do it without even thinking about it consciously. All the habits we learn, from brushing our teeth to driving a car, are automatic habits that we have developed unconscious competence for.

Here's the important thing to remember: some people might take more naturally to driving a car, having a particular genetic predisposition to being great at driving; but anyone can learn to be great in a car—maybe not as great as an Ayrton Senna or a Michael Schumacher, but they can learn to be really, really good. And that's true of every skill and every characteristic. If you practise it enough you develop unconscious competence and then it becomes automatic and even natural to you.

I believe that we're on this planet to do two things: to be impacted by the world and to make an impact on the world. We're impacted when we grow and improve as a result of how the world affects us. We impact the world by learning to apply what we've learnt to others. This is how to think about charisma. You may never speak like John F. Kennedy or Martin Luther King, but you can learn to communicate with far more impact than you do right now. You can learn to be better. It all begins with attitude.

Part 1

Step up: The attitude of charisma

Attitude is more important than facts. It is more important than the past, than education, money, circumstances, than failures and success, than what other people think, say, or do. It is more important than appearance, ability, or skill.

CHARLES R. SWINDOLL

I couldn't take my eyes off the television: a volcano grounding all Irish and British flights! You must be kidding me. Especially one from poor old Iceland, a country that had already got some of the blame for the recession. Now here they were again, this time unleashing a volcano on the rest of Europe. Iceland was like the defender who kept scoring own goals.

It was 15 April 2010 and the volcano Eyjafjallajökull had just erupted. There I was in a hotel in Manchester, about to get a taxi to go to the airport. It was 10 a.m. and I needed to get to Rome for an important conference the next day. Then I needed to be back in Dublin a couple of days later. I couldn't afford to miss either appointment.

I watched in horror as the news headline read: 'All flights grounded in the UK and Ireland until further notice.' I had to think quick, and so began a journey I would never forget. Over the next few days I made it to Rome and all the way back to Dublin by way of fourteen trains, two buses, two boats, three taxis and one hitched ride. Along the way I was told 'No' many times and informed that there was no way I would manage to get where I wanted to go and that everywhere was sold out. And yet somehow I made it. 'How?' you might ask. Simple. It was all about attitude.

As far as I was concerned I needed to get where I was going and I was going to do whatever it took to get there. Rejection didn't bother me. Failing to find the right solution didn't bother me. Looking silly didn't bother me. I was focused on one single objective: to get where I wanted to go. My attitude was that I was going to do that. I was going to get there. I was certain of it.

Along the way, I hitched a lift across borders, blagged my way onto booked-out trains and talked my way into getting special treatment. In all, I booked maybe two trains in advance. I made it in time for both conferences. When I arrived home, something struck me. The people I've met who do have that attitude also tend to be really successful. Now, of course, I'm not suggesting that you break the law or do anything illegal along your way. I'm talking about having the attitude that says 'I can, I will, let's go.' Many of the most successful people in the world have faced a lot of adversity on their way to success, and it was their attitude that carried them through.

In his biography of Steve Jobs, Walter Isaacson talks about Steve's 'reality-distortion field'. When Steve was convinced about something, even if it seemed impossible he was able to convince everyone else that it was possible. He had a remarkable ability to get others to believe him. How did he do it? It was really because of his attitude. He was convinced, so he could convince.

When I was watching the Olympics and Paralympics in 2012 two moments stood out for me. In the Olympics, of course, watching our Irish hero Katie Taylor winning the gold medal in fantastic fashion was a memorable occasion, and in the Paralympics, Jason Smyth, a runner who suffers from Stargardt's disease and has impaired vision, won gold in the 100-metre and 200-metre sprints for the second time in a row.

Both events made me very proud. Both were quite emotional. As they stepped up on the podium to receive their medals, I felt it was a perfect metaphor for what they have achieved. For it is in stepping up in the first place that these amazing athletes managed to push past their limits and become world champions multiple times. Heroes. In fact, regardless of the gold medal, everyone competing in such events is a hero in my book. Not because of what they've achieved. Not because of qualifying. Not even because they've triumphed in the face of great adversity. But because they're doing their best to live up to their best. They're practising the disciplines required to live fully.

When I talk about stepping up I'm really talking about deciding to live up to one's potential. That means being all that you're capable of being. From a charisma standpoint it means being as charismatic a communicator as you can possibly be. Because in order to do that you need to start with belief—belief in yourself, belief in your ability to impact people, belief in you being able to handle failure or rejection, belief in your ability to feel how you want to feel.

The beliefs you hold about yourself can limit you or empower you. It's important to get to know yourself, to get to like yourself and to learn a valuable lesson from babies and toddlers: that failure, rejection and embarrassment are nothing to be afraid of. Indeed, when we can come to the place where we no longer fear these things and can build the kind of feelings we want, we will be in a frame of mind that will allow us to impact others, powerfully. It's time to step up. Your attitude holds the key.

Chapter 2
The attitude factor

If you don't get everything you want, think of the things you don't get that you don't want.

OSCAR WILDE

I f there's one thing everybody who studies success takes for granted, it's the undeniable reality that your attitude has a huge impact on your success. This is true in every aspect of life, from serious business to loving relationships, from personal goals to professional sport.

Your attitude determines how you handle what happens and what you do as a result of what happens. It filters your world in such a way that it frames every event in either a useful or an unhelpful way. The process of taking charge of your life and changing the way you think, feel and behave starts at the attitude level.

When I talk about attitude I think it's important to put it into context and explain what I mean. I want you to think about your attitude as being the way you think and feel about yourself, others and the world. I want you to think about it also as the combined beliefs you hold about your life and how the world works.

Now, most people have this idea that all you need is a 'positive attitude' and your life will turn round. I disagree. I think you need a particular type of positive attitude. The 'positivity tribe', as I call it, is the emergence of coaches and trainers in the personal-development world who promote themselves as phenomenal performance experts. It seems that anyone who has read a few books or done a course can automatically become a guru. The internet enables people to market themselves powerfully to the world without having to live up to their own cultivated reputation.

As a result their advice is usually a distorted version of what they've heard their own favourite guru or author say. Sometimes it can be beneficial, but often it can take away from the effectiveness of the approach. One common meme that sprang into life and received global attention was the 'law of attraction'. It was popularised by a book by Rhonda Byrne called *The Secret*, which involved some heavy-hitters in the personal-development arena explaining how the law worked.

Now, this law is pretty simple: you get more of what you focus on. So, focus on good thoughts of what you want to attract and you will. Most of the book repeated that idea and connected with the aspirations of the reader by suggesting that achieving their goals is a lot easier than they thought. This also became a springboard for the positivity tribe to emerge with various versions of the same message: be positive—it's good for you!

The reality is that things don't work as simply as that. I know because I've imagined being a multibillionaire, with Rachel McAdams waiting for me at home every day, and, sadly, it hasn't happened yet. You see, focusing on what you want and being positive is extremely important, but it's not the only important thing. To achieve anything in life you need a few more things.

You need to start with this goal-oriented perspective. The reason *The Secret* has a lot of merit is that focusing on what you want tends to make you more likely to get it. With respect to the very funny and clever Oscar Wilde quotation above, in reality it's really important to avoid thinking about what you don't want and to switch your way of thinking around. Once you do that the next step is to figure out what challenges might stop you getting what you want. Next, find out what resources are at your disposal. Then it's about figuring out a strategy to overcome the challenges and get it. Lastly, it's about taking action and following through on your strategy.

To me the attitude to have when seeking to improve in any area of your life is that it's possible and will require effort but will most likely be worth it. When you face problems, your attitude must be dedicated to exploring what the solutions are, immediately. Many people allow themselves to dwell on their problems and the hopelessness of the situation, thereby restricting themselves to time spent ruminating on how things should be, rather than how they could be. When you immediately ask yourself, 'What's the solution?' your brain will start to figure out the various options instantly.

Our beliefs reflect what we think is true. When you think certain things are true it enables you to perform more effectively.

Unfortunately, when you have certain limiting beliefs they can prevent you being as charismatic as you can be. For example, sometimes people believe that they're not a 'people person' or that they're a 'nervous person', or that they're 'just not good at presentations'. The problem is that believing these things actually makes them more likely to be true. So if you believe that you're not a 'people person' you're more likely to shy away from being in the presence of other people—which will result in you seeming not to be a 'people person'.

An old adage states, 'Whatever the thinker thinks, the prover proves.' This means that inside our head we have certain thoughts that we think and believe, and we set ourselves up to prove these thoughts and beliefs right. So the viewpoint from which we see a situation will determine how we represent it. Whatever focus you have—something that is brought about by your beliefs—will determine how something affects you. This is known as the 'confirmation bias'.

Not only do our beliefs affect our behaviours, but our behaviours then serve to reinforce these limiting beliefs. Once we believe we're nervous, that belief causes us to act nervously, so that ultimately our beliefs about ourselves being nervous are reinforced. In psychology this is known as having 'self-efficacy beliefs'. The good news, however, is that we can have positive self-efficacy beliefs that actually serve to help us improve.

Once we begin to engage in more useful beliefs we begin to take more useful and positive actions. These actions, in turn, serve to convince us that the beliefs were right in the first place. This works because of another very interesting phenomenon of the human mind known as 'cognitive dissonance', a term coined by Leon Festinger in 1956. In short, this theory states that when our beliefs and behaviours don't match, or when they seem to be contradictory, we're in a state of cognitive dissonance. Now, we can't stay in a state of cognitive dissonance for too long, and eventually either our beliefs change by adapting to our behaviour or our behaviour adapts to our beliefs.

What we're looking for here is for our beliefs and behaviours to change and come into alignment with each other. Without charismatic beliefs you won't maintain the charismatic behaviours for long, and having charismatic beliefs doesn't guarantee that you will behave charismatically. So beliefs and behaviours are equally important.

Carol Dweck, a psychologist at Columbia University, New York, found that people generally hold one or other of two types of belief about their intelligence. Some believe that it's predetermined and others that it's malleable. When she offered students at the University of Hong Kong the opportunity to improve their English she found that the applicants had something in common: they all believed they could improve their intelligence in this area. She found that those who believed that intelligence isn't malleable avoided trying to improve it.

It's highly probable that something similar is true about charisma. If you don't believe that you can do anything about it, you will more than likely prove yourself correct. There are plenty of sceptics who regard anything remotely connected to positive thinking or self-improvement as rubbish. Many of them have a certain mindset about what is and isn't possible. You can show them the evidence of neuro-plasticity and explain how the brain circuitry is affected by the way in which we think. You can show them exactly how it works. But still they will shake their heads and cite the various over-the-top examples of positive-thinking stupidity that are everywhere.

Sceptics tend to believe one of the biggest logical fallacies going: 'association fallacy', or guilt by association. Their attitude seems to be that, because there are cranks and hoaxers in the field of self-improvement, the whole area is a cesspool of marketing scam artists and brainless boneheads. Tarring every idea in the field with the same brush serves to maintain their one-dimensional focus on the predetermined nature not just of intelligence or charisma but of our mental and emotional well-being.

The attitude that needs to be incorporated by anyone who wants to become a much more engaging and charismatic communicator is that you can improve. You can improve how you think. You can improve your mood. You can improve your behaviours. You can improve your skills. It's not a case of wishing on a star, nor is it a case of asking the universe: it's about being disciplined enough to practise thinking, acting and communicating in new ways.

It's essential for us to have specific beliefs that aid and assist the development of our personal charisma. Most people who possess good personal charisma have beliefs that enable them to behave in the most useful ways. I've distilled the key beliefs of personal charisma into the list in the following chapter. I call these the beliefs of charisma.

Chapter 3
The ten beliefs of world-class communicators

Man often becomes what he believes himself to be.
MAHATMA GANDHI

When I created the idea of the Charisma Bootcamp, one idea in particular got me excited. A friend of mine, Ruairi O'Connor, is one of Ireland's top magicians, having performed for a vast number of people, including Westlife and U2. Ruairi is an extremely likeable guy, and his job involves walking up to strangers and building a connection with them instantly. He has done that with literally hundreds of thousands of people since he started performing.

Understanding how Ruairi thinks about approaching so many people was intriguing to me. From his attitude towards such interactions we can learn so much about how to be at our best when we meet others for the first time.

Indeed, without doubt one of the best approaches to learning about brilliant communication in general is to study what the very best communicators already do. I've been lucky to have had the opportunity to work with some fantastically effective speakers, presenters, gurus, entertainers and salespeople, to name but a few. In doing so, one of the things I've discovered is that their ability to impact people doesn't necessarily begin with how they speak or what they do: it begins with how they think about interactions.

After hundreds of hours and many thousands of miles studying the best communicators I could find, I've examined their beliefs about themselves, about other people and about communication in general. I began to code the various attitudes and beliefs and eventually found a number of recurring beliefs shared by the very best at communicating, including Ruairi. After all this research, I identified ten particular beliefs that seem to be the cornerstone of effective communication. If we believe them, or presuppose that they're true, we will be more likely to make a better impression on others. These beliefs represent things we assume about the world in order to be charismatic.

1. There is no such thing as failure, only feedback

This belief is simply the most useful way of thinking about 'failure'. Remember, failure is a concept that was created by someone at some time in the past. It doesn't actually exist.

All that happens when you 'fail' is that you don't happen to get the result you wanted. Instead, you get a different result. Therefore you simply receive the information that what you did didn't work and that you need to try something else.

Failure is just feedback that can help you become more successful, and every time you don't succeed is a rare and unprecedented opportunity to learn something new.

2. Rejection is the other person's problem: it means nothing and just explains their present perception and agenda

Rejection is simply information about another person's perspective or circumstances. It means nothing about who you are or how good or valuable you are. Instead, it reveals that their perspective is not accepting of you or what you seem to be offering. The truth is that the other person often has very little information about what you offer, and they rely on this small amount to make their judgement.

Even in cases where a person is rejected by a long-term romantic partner, it's still not fully dependent on that person's perspective, because the mechanics of love and the process of falling in and out of it with different people affect how the other person sees you and distort their point of view. When you fall in love with someone, chemicals such as oxytocin and phenethylamine cloud your reasoning, and you tend to see that person with few faults. When you fall out of love, the change in neurochemistry often causes you to feel the exact opposite. Neither of these emotional states allows you to be rational about the qualities of the other person. Indeed, as a friend, you get to see the other person with their good and bad points, and you're in a far better position to evaluate them.

3. Embarrassment and awkwardness exist only in the mind—they are a choice

Embarrassment and awkwardness can only happen when you create these states within yourself. You can do something ridiculous and feel comfortable or you can do something ridiculous and feel embarrassed. The choice, ultimately, is yours. You can feel awkward around others or feel comfortable around them. Again, it's up to you.

The key is to remember this and to make sure when you're in situations that would have made you feel awkward or embarrassed in the past to deliberately feel as comfortable as you can. When you stay in this state you will eliminate the possibility of feeling in any way awkward.

4. Seriousness is a disease that can be cured by laughter

A big secret to achieving happy, wonderful, effective communication with others is remembering the importance of laughter. Being able to laugh at situations and find the funny side of life are key ingredients in getting on brilliantly with people and in being the kind of person others like being around. The best communicators often also have the best sense of humour. Indeed, Richard Bandler, probably the most charismatic person I've ever met, describes seriousness as one of the biggest diseases that people have.

5. Charisma is an impression that can be turned up or turned down

We don't just walk round with the same 'amount' of charisma in how we come across to others throughout each day. We have lots of potential, and we realise more of this potential at different times. Once you learn about how you can create and cultivate more charisma you can discover how to turn your charisma up and down at will. Not every situation requires you to stand out and captivate other people.

6. You're not what you do—you're everything you can become at your very best

It's important never to limit people by their behaviours. What happens too often is that we think behaving in a certain way makes us a particular kind of person. When, instead, you realise that you're the kind of person who can do so much more than you ever thought possible, you can get on with enjoying doing things and taking actions that enable you to do better in life.

7. If you want to get what you want, you need to let go of needing it

In psychology there is what is known as the 'law of reversed effort'. It states that the harder you try to do something, the harder it is. So the harder you try to fall asleep, the more awake you feel; the harder you try to stop panicking, the more you panic. The key is to remember that you have to learn to be okay in the face of the worst-case scenario. Once you do this you will no longer need the best-case scenario to happen: you will simply want it to, and you will make it much more likely to happen. Now, of course, putting in the effort is essential to achievement. The problem comes when you feel like you 'need' something in order to be happy. This state of neediness leads you to push away whatever it is. If you're needy with other people they will be repelled. The solution is to desire what you want and to be prepared to work hard for it but at the same time to realise that without it you're still okay.

8. Silence can speak when you let it

You can't not communicate: everything you do or don't do communicates to another person. Keeping this in mind, when you're silent, other people will develop an impression of you and what the silence means.

It's important that you control what the silence means, because if you don't others will—and they may not do it in the most useful ways.

9. Get on better with yourself and you'll get on better with everyone else

Getting on with people starts with getting on with yourself. When you're good to yourself you practise being good to others. More importantly, when you're happy with yourself you feel really good, and that puts you in the best state to be with other people.

10. You define who you are—you define what you do—you define how you live

It's really important to remember that you have control over the way you think about yourself. Most people don't realise that they run their own brain. Once you understand this you can ensure that you put your brain into practice and begin to use it deliberately to enhance the quality of your life.

THE 'CHARISMATIC BELIEFS' EXERCISE
Go through each of these ten beliefs and identify key areas in your life
where you're going to use each belief to improve your experience.

1. There is no such thing as failure, only feedback.

_____

_____

_____

_____

_____

_____

2. Rejection is the other person's problem: it means nothing and just
    explains their present perception and agenda.

_____

_____

_____

_____

_____

3. Embarrassment and awkwardness only exist in the mind—they
    are a choice.

_____

_____

_____

_____

_____

4. Seriousness is a disease that can be cured by laughter.

_____

_____

_____

_____

5.   Charisma is an impression that can be turned up or turned down.

_____
_____
_____
_____
_____
_____

6.   You're not what you do—you're everything you can become at your very best.

_____
_____
_____
_____
_____
_____

7.   If you want to get what you want, you need to let go of needing it.

_____
_____
_____
_____
_____
_____

8.   Silence can speak when you let it.

_____
_____
_____
_____
_____
_____

9. Get on better with yourself and you'll get on better with everyone
    else.

    _____

    _____

    _____

    _____

    _____

    _____

10. You define who you are—you define what you do—you define
    how you live.

    _____

    _____

    _____

    _____

    _____

    _____

Chapter 4
Getting to know yourself

You need to know things the others don't know. It's what no one knows about you that allows you to know yourself.

DON DELILLO

Imagine you walk into a room and are greeted by yourself—that you meet yourself and shake your hand. Imagine you can chat with yourself and, as you do, notice how you come across and what kind of person you are. Imagine you get to talk deeply with yourself and explore your good points and bad points, your beliefs and values, the incidents that have made you the person you are today. This is an incredibly rewarding experience.

Far too often, because we're too close to ourselves it's difficult to get a fresh and unbiased viewpoint on who we are. The first thing we need to do when beginning to take control of our beliefs about ourselves is to understand how we think about ourselves at the moment. Here I want to introduce you to a particular way of thinking that I learnt to use and that helped me to improve how I felt about myself.

The 'character model' is what I developed to study the self. When I researched all the ways of looking at the 'problems of the self', I discovered that everything had been made far too complicated. I developed a way to examine the self that would encompass the main problems that existed and teach people how they could deal with them effectively and simply. Furthermore, this new way laid the foundation for enabling people to enhance their charisma.

In becoming more charismatic, it's essential that you start by becoming more aware of the way you think about yourself. Building a strong character, however, is crucial in order to be the kind of person you project to the world. Let me clarify some terms.

Your *identity* is the way you think about yourself. It's made up of the way you see yourself (self-image), think about yourself (self-concept) and feel about yourself (self-esteem).

Your *reputation* is how others think of you.

The *impression* you make on others is how you affect your reputation.

Your *personality* is the generalisation made about you according to your preferences, beliefs and consistent behaviours.

Your *character* is who you are, deep down. It's the seat of your values and best self.

These terms are relevant because it's important that you develop the most useful identity and perspective of yourself. That way you can go on and learn to control the kinds of impression you make on other people. This, in turn, will enable you to have some power to affect how they construct your personality to themselves; therefore you can construct yourself as being charismatic. It's important that you start with your identity, because otherwise you will simply be putting on an act. It's crucial for you to realise that you have so much charismatic potential.

You get signs of your potential when you're in certain situations. There are particular people with whom you feel more charismatic and others with whom you don't. Now, instead of wondering what the difference is in relation to 'why' you feel differently in either situation, the key is to understand how to come across more charismatically in both situations. Once you've developed a more useful identity you will be able to feel like a more charismatic person, and that will enable you to behave more charismatically. It becomes a self-fulfilling prophecy.

It's also important to recognise that you're always much more than your individual behaviours. Far too often we limit ourselves and explain that we're just 'this kind of person' or 'that kind of person', when in reality it's simply a pattern of behaviour we got into or a belief we adopted. For example, if we fail at something it's all too easy to state that we're just 'not any good at it'. That lets us off the hook in our own lovely fortress of dismal self-pity. The reality is that if we try something and fail, all we know is that there are things we must learn in order to become good at it.

Take learning a foreign language. I know many people who have begun a foreign-language course but don't feel as if they're improving. Crucially, when they have an opportunity to practise their skills they don't—in case they get it wrong. Yet the only way to learn anything is to practise, to make some mistakes, to get some things right and then to learn the difference. You need to be willing to make mistakes to become skilled at anything.

So we are not who we think we are and we are not the behaviours we engage in or the mistakes we make. We are absolutely everything we can become at our best. This perspective I'm talking about refers to the concept of character. Deep down, all the potential you have exists in your character, and that's the true person that you are. Once you understand this, it helps you shift dramatically from all the needless insecurities and doubts you can have about yourself when you consider your identity.

Building character is really about revealing character. I believe that your best self is your character and that you unveil it when you respond as well as you possibly can to what life throws at you. You see, we attempt to discover who we are by studying what we do, what we believe and who we seem to be to others. This can be confusing, as we're often very different to different people and in different contexts. You act differently with your mother or father from how you act with your husband or wife (at least I sincerely hope you do!).

So, with this confusion, we're left in a state of doubt about our 'true personality' or 'true identity'. Sometimes people even go so far as to embark on a spiritual retreat, to India for example, in an attempt to 'find themselves' and 'discover who they truly are'. The key, though, is to remember that who you truly are is simple: you truly are the best possible self you can be.

Even when your personality changes, your goodness as a person does not. Even when your behaviour changes, your values and principles do not. Even when your actions change, the very best version of you does not. Who you are at your best is always the same. You, as the very best father or mother you can be, is the same as you as the very best lover or friend you can be. It's still you being yourself fully and impacting others in the most powerful way you can. The key is to start being that best version of yourself more and more.

Now, unfortunately, because we're human beings we're one of the few species that don't always live up to their potential. For example, trees don't half-grow; they grow as tall as they can. Ants don't sort of work; they work as hard as they can. Most species live as much as it's possible to live and reach their full potential. They don't 'show character' like we do sometimes. They are their 'character'.

We show character most often in times of crisis or when we're under pressure. For some reason, when we have to we gain a phenomenal ability to reach our potential. Now, when I'm talking about potential I'm also aware of its changing nature. For example, I may ask you today to play the guitar as well as you can. However, even if you do, tomorrow your potential will increase and you will play better. So potential is not something we can actively measure. The good news, though, is that we don't have to measure it: we simply have to know that it exists. Once we know that, it gives us the ability to perform and become much better than we are at any moment in time. You see, when you begin to act more like you are at your best, you will naturally start to become more charismatic.

Being your character more often means fulfilling your potential to a greater extent. So the closer you can align your character (who you really are: you at your best) and your identity (who you think you are), the better you will be at thinking in more useful ways, and the more likely it will be that you will fulfil more of your potential.

It's also vital to be aware of the important keys to being able to change your identity. Since identity reflects who you see yourself as, who you think you are and how you feel about yourself, these are the three areas that can change.

THE 'IDENTITY' EXERCISE

Look in the mirror. Who do you see yourself as?

_____
_____
_____
_____
_____
_____

Listen to your voice played back to you on a recorder. Who do you sound like you are?

_____
_____
_____
_____
_____
_____

What do you think about yourself?

_____
_____
_____
_____
_____
_____

How do you feel about yourself?

_____
_____
_____
_____
_____
_____

The combination of these answers reflects your identity—how you think about yourself. Now that you're aware of that, it's time to examine your character.

THE 'TRUE CHARACTER' EXERCISE
What is most important to you in your life?

_____
_____
_____
_____
_____
_____

What are the most important qualities you value as a person?

_____
_____
_____
_____
_____
_____

What are the five things you've done that you're most proud of?

_____
_____
_____
_____
_____
_____

What are you best at?

_____
_____
_____
_____
_____

Who are you at your absolute best?

_____
_____
_____
_____
_____

What do you look like at your best?

_____

_____

_____

_____

_____

_____

How do you sound at your best?

_____

_____

_____

_____

_____

_____

What do you think of yourself at your absolute best?

_____

_____

_____

_____

_____

_____

How do you feel about yourself at your best?

_____

_____

_____

_____

_____

_____

What is possible at your best?

_____

_____

_____

_____

_____

_____

What stops you from being at your best more often?

_____

_____

_____

_____

_____

_____

What would happen if you were at your best more often in the future?

_____

_____

_____

_____

_____

What do you need to do to start acting at your best now?

_____

_____

_____

_____

_____

Now, examine what you've written. You've now answered important questions that reveal a lot about you. The next step is to examine your answers and choose who you're going to decide to be.

Chapter 5

The strength of your character

It ain't what they call you, it's what you answer to.

W. C. FIELDS

It was actually a film that changed my life—a film that ignited the flame of determination that burned inside me. In those days, when I regularly contemplated suicide, one night after school, after a particularly bad day, I lay at home in bed watching my small black-and-white television. Having finished my homework, I found myself hurt and alone. Again, I was crying; again, I was in severe emotional pain. Then *Rocky* came on.

It seems silly, but as it began I felt myself transported into the film, experiencing life as this loser, has-been boxer, Rocky Balboa, written off by everyone as living a 'nothing' life. I found myself relating to what it felt like. I too was a loser, a reject. I too was looked down on by others. I too was pathetic.

But I too had more inside me than anyone knew.

This classic film chronicles the journey of a nobody who gets the chance to be somebody. It looks at how he was 'down and out', living a mediocre existence. It explores his struggle to get fit enough and good enough to compete. It examines his self-doubt. It reveals his desire to fight, to do his best, to be his best. It shows his character.

He goes on to fight the champion of the world, Apollo Creed, and, miraculously, lasts far longer than anyone expected. In the second-last round, there's an incredible scene. Rocky, still fighting his heart out, looks tired and spent. You see him taking punch after punch, hit after hit. He stumbles but stays upright. The crowd gets louder. There's a barrage of punches and, finally, he gets knocked down by the champion.

The commentator screams as Rocky scrambles. You see him down and out after a war of a fight, clambering hopelessly to get up as his trainer, Mickey, shouts to him to stay down for fear of getting too badly hurt.

The referee begins his count, '1 . . . 2 . . . 3 . . .' I'm holding my breath, calling out, *'Get up, Rocky. Get up! C'mon! You can do it!'* I scream. I will him to stand with every fibre of my being. The referee continues, '4 . . . 5 . . . 6 . . .' *'C'mon, Rocky. Fight. Get up and fight. You can do it.'* Every punch he takes is the bullying that hurts me. Every strike is another friend who betrays me. *'Come on!'* The knock down is the culmination of all the pain. '7 . . . 8 . . . 9 . . .'

And then something incredible happens: Rocky gets to his feet. Apollo looks shocked. Rocky stands up, bruised and battered, ready to continue. There's blood everywhere. He looks broken but for his spirit, and his will takes him on. He keeps fighting.

Every time I see that scene and hear the music every hair stands up at the back of my neck, and I find myself welling up. You see, I was Rocky. And Rocky was me. At that moment I decided I would dig deeper than ever, find more strength than ever and pick myself back up off the ground of depression, and I wouldn't stop. I would find my character and step up to being who I was born to be. And that was the moment my life changed.

It's usually in the toughest times that we find our true character. The challenges you've been through have shown you who you are. For it is of your triumphs against adversity that you can be most proud. Once you acknowledge that inside you lies such incredible power and strength, the next step is to examine how you are 'being' in different areas of your life.

THE DEFINITION OF YOU

Many people seek to define themselves in a particular way. The kind of person you are depends on how you decide to define yourself, on what kind of meaning you tend to ascribe to yourself.

You see, we're all meaning-making beings. We construct meanings out of our experiences, and these meanings explain our experiences. We seem to need meanings to function effectively in the world. This is important because most meanings we construct for ourselves are not necessarily relevant or accurate in any way. Instead, they cause us to act in certain ways.

When you're asked the question 'Who are you?' it's really another way of saying 'What do *you* mean?' The way in which you come across means that you will be a different person to different people. So the important question to answer is 'How do you come across to the various people in your life?' When you answer this question, you will learn much about yourself, as well as about what you need to do to come across more effectively and create a better impression on other people.

Whatever meaning you have ascribed to yourself and whatever way you defined yourself, it's essential to ask yourself, 'How are you behaving in the different contexts of your life?' This exercise is about focusing on which traits you seem to be revealing in the different roles you fulfil in your life. Once you become aware of which traits are displayed in which aspects of life, you will get a better understanding of how you can more usefully come across to others in the various contexts and roles you act out.

The following exercise is borrowed from my friend and colleague Brian Colbert and the excellent work in his best-selling book *The Happiness Habit*.

THE 'ROLES' EXERCISE
What kind of person are you?

_____

_____

_____

_____

_____

_____

What kind of person does a new acquaintance think you are?

_____

_____

_____

_____

_____

Who do your friends think you are?

_____
_____
_____
_____
_____
_____

Who do your colleagues think you are?

_____
_____
_____
_____
_____
_____

Who does your family think you are?

_____
_____
_____
_____
_____
_____

How do you want your family to describe you?

_____
_____
_____
_____
_____
_____

How do you want your friends to describe you?

_____
_____
_____
_____
_____

How do you want your colleagues to describe you?

_____

_____

_____

_____

_____

_____

How do you want a new acquaintance to describe you?

_____

_____

_____

_____

_____

_____

CHARISMATIC PHILOSOPHY

Once you understand how you act in the various roles of life, you will know which relationships you most need to work. In order to live as your best self in those roles, it's also a good idea to develop what I call a 'charismatic philosophy'.

A charismatic philosophy is about looking at life and the world from the viewpoint that accepts your wonderfulness as a person and all the potential that exists inside you. Since you're not what you do but everything you can become, it's important to remember the elements given below in relation to knowing who you truly are and to concentrate on improving and developing each quality to help you reach more and more of your potential. Once you do this you will find yourself living a more charismatic life.

The character elements I describe in the special paragraphs that follow are positive, useful traits that you can focus on developing. After defeating the enemies of charisma with your new-found attitude to the fears you used to have, the next step is to focus on developing your character as far as possible. So, what is the truth about you?

You are wise and you are knowledgeable. You are creative and original and have moments of genius. You are curious and open-minded and have good judgement. You are great at learning and love doing it. You can see things from different points of view. You are courageous and brave, confident and strong. You are flexible, persevering and persistent, determined and motivated. You are inspiring and full of integrity, honour, honesty and kindness. You are compassionate, genuine and generous, and you have a good heart. You have a good sense of fairness, equality and humanity. You have great energy and are cheerful and hopeful, and you look forward to the future optimistically.

You are a great leader, you have fantastic self-control and you have a great sense of gratitude and appreciation for all of your life. You have a great sense of humour and you love your life. You love yourself and have lots of love in your life, and you have an amazing capacity to love and be loved. You connect with others brilliantly and have wonderful social skills. You do your best every single day at whatever you do. In short, you are absolutely phenomenal.

Now, the good news: even if you don't think this describes you fairly, it's absolutely true. This is you—who you are at your absolute best. So any time you ask yourself the question 'Who am I?' read my answer, as it's the closest thing you'll get to the truth.

Here's the catch and the even better news: every one of the traits I've listed is one you can improve on and develop. How do you love yourself? Act in a loving way to yourself. How do you act courageously? Act in the face of fear. How do you become wise? Learn constantly. Stop and ask yourself this question for each of these traits: 'What do I need to do in order to develop that trait?' Your answer reveals actions you can take to become the best person you can be. Think about it. There has been at least one time when you've demonstrated every quality I've mentioned. Now, if you've done it once you can do it again . . . and again . . . and again. Then you will know what it's like to be living your potential.

From this place, then, a charismatic philosophy is a natural by-product, for when you are living your potential and are your 'best self', you will truly present yourself in the most charismatic way. Then you have to get to learn to like yourself.

Chapter 6
How to like yourself

To love oneself is the beginning of a lifelong romance.

OSCAR WILDE

Every morning, before I leave my apartment, I have a ritual. I look in the mirror and say to myself out loud, 'My god, you're gorgeous. Those lucky people out there are going to get to see your handsome face.' Now, this is not a case of being arrogant or egotistical, nor is it an example of me reminding myself that it's actually true. (Of course, it would be nice if you, the reader, thought it was true, and if you do, please contact me and let me know . . . If you don't, then please keep your opinions to yourself!)

The reason I do it is that it makes me smile, and by complimenting myself I feel better about myself. Even when I wake up in the morning and look terrible and my hair is all over the place and I look like a ghost, I still look at myself in the mirror and say to myself, 'You do look pretty rough at the moment, but deep down we both know you're gorgeous.' This starts my day in a wonderful way. Nobody else has to know. It's the first example of me being good to myself.

I buy myself presents regularly. I make time to do things I want to do. I give myself the odd treat. I encourage myself when I make mistakes or when I'm going through hard times. I remind myself of everything I've achieved. I recall memories that make me feel good. I'm really kind to myself, and because of that I'm very comfortable in my own company. This has meant that, wherever I've gone, all over the world, people have approached me and wanted to get to know me without me even uttering a word. When you feel good about who you are, people will feel good around you.

To me, this is absolutely critical in becoming more charismatic.

You have to like and love yourself. For anyone else to feel comfortable around you, you need to feel comfortable with yourself. When you like yourself, it makes it easier for other people to like you too.

There are plenty of self-help books that talk about liking yourself and loving yourself, but very few, if any, actually explain how you can do just this. I spent much of my teenage years wanting to be somebody I felt I was not, and I went through a phase where I felt I was faking everything. When I acted confidently, I felt self-doubt lurking inside me, telling me that things weren't going to work out and warning me that I would fail and that I wasn't good enough.

We have the expression 'I said to myself . . .' It's always occurred to me that this expression means that there are at least two selves within us. Freud came up with the concept of the id, the ego and the superego. These were different parts of who we are. We had our instinctive selves, our functional selves and our morally conscious selves. Although I never liked this particular model, I do believe in the notion that we have different selves, and at least two of them.

This, of course, doesn't mean that we have multiple personalities in the sense of psychological disorder. It simply means that inside us we often have conversations going on in which we ask and answer questions and in which we praise and criticise ourselves. People who are depressed often have a voice inside their head that's too critical, negative and insulting. That voice is often stronger and clearer than any others. When someone is depressed, this voice takes control and undermines every positive step they might try to take. Whenever a person learns through NLP or cognitive behavioural therapy to overcome depression, one of the most important things they learn is how to handle this voice.

We develop habitual behaviours and thought patterns inside our head that cause us to feel bad. Often, this kind of voice hacks away at everything we feel good about. To become happier with yourself the first thing that has to happen is that this voice needs to be stopped in its tracks.

Every time we learn to do something we make a connection inside our brains. When we practise this action, we strengthen this connection. This is how learning takes place and how habits are formed. The only way to block a habit is to replace it with a new habit. This means we must learn how to develop a new habitual pattern of thinking.

THE 'MANTRA' EXERCISE

For us to do this, it's important to interrupt the old pattern and stop it from working in the first place. My mentor, Richard Bandler, shared with me a wonderful trick for doing this. I've used this with almost everyone I've ever worked with, and when they've done it they've reported it as being one of the most successful techniques they've ever learnt. It's known as the 'mantra'.

One version of this mantra that I use involves taking a time when you find yourself giving out to yourself, criticising yourself, undermining yourself or in any way using the negative voice to make yourself feel bad and doing something about it. You think in this usual negative way and then you begin to repeat in a strong tone of voice the mantra 'Shut up now, shut up now, shut up now'.

This works because you're giving a firm, direct command to your brain, ordering it to stop each time it's negative. Every time the negative voice begins, you use this mantra, and pretty soon you learn not to play out the negative voice. You condition your brain to stop doing what it was doing. This gives you a chance to put different ideas and suggestions in there.

THE 'RIDICULE' EXERCISE

Another way to tackle the negative voice is this: the next time you find yourself criticising yourself, say something out loud—obviously not publicly—and exaggerate your tone of voice until it becomes ridiculous. So if you're saying, 'I'm so stupid,' repeat it, 'I'm ssoooooooooooooo stuuuuuuuuuuuuupppppppiiiiiiiddddddd', over and over again in a ridiculous voice. What this does is associate ridiculousness with what the voice says, so that you no longer take it seriously.

Once you've learnt to stop the negative voice and thought patterns inside your head, you can begin to communicate with yourself in a much more useful way. You need not only to say nice things to yourself but to say them with certainty in a nice tone of voice. It's time to start speaking to yourself as your own motivational coach.

You can start learning to practise the skill of liking yourself. I thought to myself for a long time, 'How can people learn to like themselves when they don't?' Then it suddenly occurred to me: liking and loving are things you do. They're behaviours. If you can learn to like and love others, you can learn to like and love yourself by doing the very same things.

Already, by realising that you are who you can be at your best, and by discovering much more about how wonderful you are compared with others, this will help you. However, to truly start liking and loving yourself as a habit it's important that you treat yourself like those in your life who you like and love.

You're the only person who will be there all the way through your life. What this means is that you can fully count only on yourself. Therefore it's vital that you become your own best friend and supporter.

How do you do that? Well, how do you like others? How do you make them feel good and like you? You're there for them. You sometimes buy them presents. You're thoughtful to them. You help them when they need a hand. You compliment them. You encourage them. What else do you do? How else do you show your love to others? Most importantly, how can you learn to do this for yourself? How can you treat yourself better? How can you be nicer to yourself? How can you say nicer things to yourself and encourage yourself more? When you begin to treat yourself better, you will begin to like yourself more. It's that simple. The nicer you are to yourself, the better you will feel about yourself, the nicer it will be to be in your own company.

There are many people who are afraid to be by themselves. They hate being alone so much that they will take up jobs they don't want to do or enter into relationships they don't want to be in, all to avoid being on their own. They hate having time by themselves because they have to spend it with themselves, and they treat themselves horribly in that time.

When you learn the skill of liking and loving yourself, something wonderful happens: you begin to discover what a great person you can really be. It makes it so much easier for other people to want to be around you, because you're happier, and people like to be around those who feel happy and who present themselves as cheerful. It means that you're free not to need anyone else and that you become a more likeable person as a result of doing more good things. It also makes the inside of your head a wonderful place to live.

THE 'LIKING YOU' EXERCISE
What presents can you buy yourself?

_____
_____
_____
_____
_____
_____

What kind of things can you say to encourage yourself whenever you make mistakes?

_____
_____
_____
_____
_____
_____

What compliments can you give yourself?

_____
_____
_____
_____
_____

Name five ways you can be kinder to yourself in your life.

_____
_____
_____
_____
_____

What are your ten best memories of you being great in some way?

_____

_____

_____

_____

_____

_____

_____

_____

_____

_____

Chapter 7
The seven keys to self-esteem

Power is being told you are not loved and not being destroyed by it.

MADONNA

Barack Obama is one of the most famous and talked-about presidents in American history. More than anyone else in the public arena he has found himself glorified by some and vilified by others. In particular, he has endured his fair share of haters. It's hard to remember anyone being despised and attacked as much as he has been in his time in office. Many will point to his policies, but the Republican Party minority leader of the US Senate, Mitch McConnell, has said his most important goal was for Obama to be a one-term president. Repeated attacks by the conservative media and a whole host of conspiracy-theory books and websites have expressed such a hatred of him that it's hard to understand where the intensity comes from.

Now, I don't want to go into the history of American politics or discuss Obama's record in office. What I'm interested in is how he seems to deal with this. Love him or loathe him, he always seems to be unruffled by the many attacks that come his way. So what does he think about such criticism? How does he handle it? Watching his projected confidence and the number of decisions he's made despite deep scrutiny, I began to wonder what kept him going.

A few days ago, while pondering this very question, I came across an article profiling him written by Michael Lewis for *Vanity Fair* entitled 'Obama's Way'. It's probably one of the most fascinating insights I've ever gained into how someone who endures so much criticism learns to deal with it. Lewis quotes Obama as saying:

> One of the things you realise fairly quickly in this job is that there
> is a character people see out there called Barack Obama. That's
> not you. Whether it's good or bad, it's not you. I learned that on
> the campaign. You have to filter stuff, but you can't filter it so
> much you live in this fantasyland.

In these few short sentences lies a powerful secret for maintaining
your self-esteem and staying confident in yourself. A brilliant strategy,
one we can all learn from, is to disassociate yourself from the person
that other people think you are.

Once you've got to know yourself and like yourself, you need to
remember that, no matter what you do, there will be haters and there
will be those who wish to take you down. In Ireland, we call them
begrudgers; in Australia and New Zealand it's known as the 'tall-
poppy syndrome'. My Japanese friends introduced me to a saying
that's quite popular in Japan: 'The nail that sticks out will get a
pounding.' Since a big part of being charismatic involves standing out,
it's very likely that when you do so you'll have to face some criticism
and similar challenges. So, taking Obama's suggestion, if you choose
to remember that whoever they're attacking is not really you but a
figment of their imagination, it will have a great impact on how you
feel about such criticism. Whoever they criticise is not you: it's their
perception of you, which is very often a completely different animal,
even if they mention you by name.

The question is: how do you filter what you hear but avoid
removing yourself too far from reality? Well, the key seems to be in
understanding a balanced view of the good and bad views of yourself,
and in extracting any feedback that you feel is relevant and useful to
you in improving. You have to know the basics of what they're saying
but not associate with it.

One of the best ambiguities I've ever heard was noted by Richard
Bandler, who talked about self-esteem being let out of a person like
steam. What I realised was that when people say they feel deflated this
metaphor fits perfectly. Similarly, I've noticed that people who are too
full of self-esteem tend to be full of hot air! But when we look more
closely at what people mean when they talk about self-esteem we can
see that it really refers to how people feel about themselves. Of

everything I've learnt to do over the years, the one I focused most on and paid most attention to was self-esteem, the reason being that I hated myself, so my 'self-esteem' was continuously low back then.

Maxwell Maltz, author of the classic book *Psycho-cybernetics*, suggests that what people need to do to feel better about themselves is to change how they think about themselves on the inside. Maltz, a former plastic surgeon, found himself changing career after noticing that the people for whom the surgery had made a difference felt better because of a shift in how they thought about themselves and not because of the way they actually looked.

I spent a lot of time asking the question 'How is it possible to build consistently high self-esteem regardless of what's going on in your life?' Answering this proved a challenging but worthwhile endeavour, for it led me to understand that there were a number of principles at work in building self-esteem. Nathaniel Branden, a Canadian psychotherapist regarded by many as the 'father of the self-esteem movement', suggests that there are six pillars to self-esteem. Being familiar with Branden's great work, including his book *The Six Pillars of Self-Esteem*, I decided, in the tradition of many great authors, to get one up on him and explain seven principles! However, I do recommend studying his work, and the following principles have indeed been influenced by his ideas.

SELF-ESTEEM FORMULA
To build a strong foundation of confidence you need to ensure that you boost your self-esteem. To do so the following seven habits are the best ones to practise:

1. Self-love (loving who you are)
Loving yourself is the first part of building a strong sense of esteem for yourself. This means actually showing love to yourself in ways suggested by the chapter you've just read. It means deliberately seeing yourself as an individual and showing some compassion to and care for yourself.

If you start to think of yourself as an important person in your life, one who will always be with you, it makes it easier to ensure that you actually start to show some love to yourself.

2. Self-acceptance (accepting your good and bad points)

Accepting yourself means looking at all your good and bad points, accepting those you can't change and working on those you can. It means accepting your weirdness or negative feelings and your failings and doing your best to overcome what you can. It means being okay with the fact that you're imperfect.

The reality is that no-one is perfect, and even though some people try to hold themselves up to such an impossible idea it's not the smartest way of thinking. A much better approach is to focus on how you can give yourself a break and be okay with the good and the bad.

3. Self-control (taking responsibility for and control over your behaviour)

Controlling yourself means taking responsibility for what you decide to do and not do. It means accepting that you have a choice, that you're the one who dictates what you're doing and are therefore in control. It means having discipline to do good and to resist temptation to do bad.

If you want to reach your goals, you have to be prepared to make sacrifices and put in deliberate effort towards taking the necessary steps. Your ability to do this and to discipline yourself when you need to will have a significant impact on the way you feel about yourself.

4. Self-assertiveness (independence, standing up for yourself)

Asserting yourself is about being independent and strong. It's about standing up for yourself. It means you're asserting what you want and what you stand for to others instead of backing down and hiding who you are.

Avoid confusing being assertive with being aggressive. Aggressiveness is when you try to intimidate others into agreeing with you. Assertiveness is when you state your argument or message in a confident way with certainty and ensure that people listen to you.

5. Self-understanding (knowing yourself and your reason for being)

Understanding yourself means knowing who you are and why you're on this earth. It means being aware of your purpose and mission and of what your values are so that you can be 100 per cent comfortable with the decisions you make in accordance with those values.

This involves looking into your values and beliefs and into what kind of person you are. Leaders and the most successful communicators seem to understand who they are and what their mission is. It's a good idea to explore this.

6. Self-belief (believing in yourself and your capabilities)
Believing in yourself means developing a sense of certainty in your own capabilities as a person. It means that you know you're the kind of person who can succeed despite any obstacle and overcome any challenge. Using intelligent self-talk and practising visualising yourself succeeding are good ways to help you develop more self-belief.

It's also a good idea to practise remembering all the times you've succeeded in the past so that they bring back a feeling of self-assuredness and recall experiences when you demonstrated your worth.

7. Self-respect (respecting yourself and acting with integrity)
Respecting yourself means treating yourself with the same level of consideration as you would others. It means avoiding berating yourself or sacrificing yourself all the time. It means doing the right thing for the right reason and being able to sleep soundly every night because of how you've acted in your life.

When you act with integrity, it gives you a sense of freedom and confidence in yourself that's based on your being a good person. It helps you feel that you're doing good and are the kind of person that makes you proud.

When I was younger, I had a bad relationship with myself. Although I feel really great about who I am now, there are times when self-doubt and insecurity creep in. Actually, it doesn't 'creep in', because 'it' isn't a thing, nor is it alive. I simply mean that I engage in self-doubting or insecuritising. (Yes, I did just make up the word 'insecuritising'.)

Anyway, even when this happens, I've found it incredibly useful to come back to these seven habits. They have become a strong foundation for me.

THE 'SELF-ESTEEM' EXERCISE

1. Self-love

How can you show love to yourself more (following on from the work in the last chapter)?

_____

_____

_____

_____

_____

_____

2. Self-acceptance

What are the best parts of you?
What are the worst parts of you?
What can you improve or change?
What can't you?

Oh, and whatever the reason, get over it!

_____

_____

_____

_____

_____

_____

3. Self-control

What are the disciplines and behaviours you're going to commit to in the future?
Why is it so important for you to commit to them?

_____

_____

_____

_____

_____

_____

4. Self-assertiveness

Who in your life do you need to stand up to in the future?
How are you going to do that?

_____

_____

_____

_____

_____

_____

5. Self-understanding

What do you value most in your life?
What do you believe about yourself?
What is your purpose in this world?
What is your mission on this planet?

_____

_____

_____

_____

_____

_____

6. Self-belief

What do you look like at your absolute best?
What kind of things would you say to yourself at your absolute best?

_____

_____

_____

_____

_____

_____

7. Self-respect

How can you make sure that every decision you make is based on doing the right thing?

_____

_____

_____

_____

_____

Chapter 8
Defeating the seven enemies of charisma

When in doubt, make a fool of yourself. There is a microscopically thin line between being brilliantly creative and acting like the most gigantic idiot on earth. So, what the hell, leap!

CYNTHIA HEIMEL

I don't have much of a problem with rejection. But there's someone I know who goes far, far beyond that. This friend has absolutely no problem whatsoever, in any way, with being rejected. For the sake of confidentiality let's call him Des (even if his real name is Damien). I'm kidding: he's not called either . . .

Not only does rejection not seem to faze Des, he actually seems to enjoy it. One night a good few years ago another friend and I went out with Des. We arrived in Dublin about 7:30 p.m. At that point my friend and I decided to play a game. With a pencil and a beer mat we began to count how many women Des approached in one evening.

Now, this guy was a machine, and since he knew what we were doing he was also showing off. From when we started counting to about 3 a.m., we counted no fewer than eighty-three women. *Eighty-three!* It was incredible. Finally, in a drunken club, he found a woman who said yes (albeit a very drunken yes). The next day when I was speaking to Des, I found myself needing to ask him a question. I couldn't understand how he didn't seem bothered at all that he got so many rejections. 'Look,' I said, 'there's something I don't get: how can you not care in any way whatsoever about all those rejections? I mean, you weren't fazed. I have to know. How do you think about those rejections? I mean, what's your explanation as to why they said no?'

He looks at me, raises his head in semi-indignation and says, 'Well, it's obvious, isn't it: they're obviously all lesbians!'

Des has an ability to find a different meaning in rejection that serves him in one sense. It enables him to maintain a strong sense of self-esteem even in the presence of such a set of responses. Now, on the other hand, his failure to take feedback means that his way of thinking doesn't necessarily serve him as well as it could. But the fact remains that he learnt to reframe and redefine what rejection meant.

In many ways we can all learn from this. Although I strongly suggest that you don't take on board the same strategy, I do recommend redefining what rejection means to you—but not just rejection. There are a number of fears and emotional states of mind that hold us back. I call these the 'enemies of charisma'.

These enemies are those problems that stop you becoming as good as you can possibly be. They may eat away at your confidence or prevent you from approaching people. They may keep you locked inside with chains of fear, insecurity and anxiety. They may make you feel shy, not good enough and unsure of yourself.

To me, there are seven enemies of personal charisma, and the vast majority of people face them to some degree. In this chapter, I want to show you ways in which you can turn your reaction to these enemies around and defeat them. These enemies are:
- fear of failure
- fear of rejection
- fear of embarrassment
- seriousness
- awkwardness
- over-analysing
- self-consciousness.

What I'm interested in doing is going through each enemy to help you completely change your attitude and the way you feel about them so that you can turn things around. Firstly, however, I want to explore two of the main causes of these enemies of charisma: caring too much about what other people think, and the nature of jealousy.

WHAT OTHER PEOPLE THINK
Caring too much about what other people think is a huge problem. I've had many clients whose biggest problem was how they felt other

people looked at them and thought of them. Our reputation has always been important to us. The problem is that we cause ourselves trouble because so often we care so much about what other people think that we become self-conscious, nervous and panicked, and we back away from doing the things that would improve our lives.

When it comes down to it, how do most of us want other people to see us? Well, I'd say this is pretty simple. We want other people to see us as smart, attractive, cool, successful and skilled. So, we develop a fear of failure because we worry that if we fail in front of others they might question our skill and intelligence. We develop a fear of rejection in case we find out that somebody thinks we're unattractive. We develop a fear of embarrassment in case we find out that somebody is laughing at us and thinks we look stupid and uncool. We take ourselves seriously because we learn to think that being 'taken seriously' is a good thing and means that we're successful. We guard our reputation in case we 'lose face'. We over-analyse everything in an attempt to ensure that everything goes perfectly and that we aren't making a mistake in our perception. We become awkward and self-conscious because we make 'how we come across' such an important thing.

We hide ourselves and exaggerate our income and possessions in case somebody sees us as not being very successful. Then, to cap it all, we might even compare ourselves to others who we consider to be better than us—all in a desire to make ourselves feel bad.

So we're left running away from what we truly want to do and running away from truly expressing ourselves, in case we make an idiot of ourselves or get rejected or embarrassed. We hide a great deal of our true selves and constantly watch our backs in an effort to survive socially.

These enemies of charisma try and protect us, but they serve to disable us. They prevent us from becoming more charismatic. They limit us in being who we truly are and who we want to be.

So, what's the solution? How do we overcome these problems? How can we still come across well to other people, or get rid of the need to do so? Let's discover how by looking at each one of these five elements.

Smart

Many people think they're smarter than everyone else; many others think they're stupid. Here's the truth: you're neither stupid nor smart, you do stupid or smart things. It's stupid to think you're smarter than everyone else or more stupid than everyone else, because it doesn't help you do anything any better. It's smart to think of yourself as a smart person who can learn and teach other smart people.

People will come up with their own perception of how smart you are. You can't really affect it that much. One good way is to be quieter around people and nod as if you understand when other people speak. People often read intelligence into silence. Most people who would think you were stupid are stupid for thinking that anyway. The smart ones are the ones who realise you're smart.

Attractive

The bottom line here is that you're attractive to some people and not to others. So the key is for you to realise that you need to do what you can to make yourself as attractive as is possible for you. Look after your body and be good to yourself, then people will make their own judgements.

You just have to be yourself. Some will like it, some won't. It's a numbers game. By looking after yourself and learning about attraction you can assist the process. By getting new clothes or following some advice from those who know what they're talking about, you will improve how attractive you are. Often it's the subtle things. It's the small details that are important.

Cool

Coolness is reflected by how relaxed and confident you seem within yourself. What some people think of as cool is someone who has other people always looking up to them and wanting to be with them. But actually, when you think about it, people who need other people to be around them all the time are steeped in insecurity.

Take going somewhere on your own. Needing others to be with you for you to feel okay reveals a lot of insecurity about yourself. Instead, if you just go on your own, when you want to go, you demonstrate an obvious confidence in yourself that makes you extremely cool.

Obviously I'm not talking about going to dangerous places on your own. I'm simply referring to how you feel when doing things by yourself. I'm talking about not paying so much attention to what you think going out on your own might say about you to other people. Actually, most people find it very appealing to see someone who doesn't seem to need company, as it shows confidence and a sense of security. That is, as long as you smile and look approachable too.

Successful

Was Mother Teresa successful? Was Gandhi? Most people would say they were, because they made an impact on the world. Whatever the impact you have on the world, when you make it you're successful.

Other people might evaluate success in terms of money, but how many financially secure people do you know who are very happy and have a great life? Probably, if you're like me, about the same number of people you know who aren't financially secure. So, really, are you going to care that much about what other people think regarding your job, career or financial situation? Financial discrimination is as ludicrous as every other kind.

Being successful means living every day as well as you can. In order to do this, you simply need to do your best and learn from your mistakes. It really is that simple.

Skilled

If you make a mistake, you make a mistake. You won't always get everything right and perfect every time. The key is to remember that everyone else is the same. When people evaluate how skilful you are they'll also be studying your attitude to the mistake.

If you have the attitude that makes it look as if you know what you're doing it doesn't matter when you make a mistake—you can see past it. However, if you let every mistake become a big deal and you continually try and defend yourself it will look like you don't know what you're doing. Besides, doing anything well is not about doing it perfectly. Again, the funny thing is that the less you try not to make mistakes, the fewer mistakes you will make.

So, in the end, what you've got to realise is that people will form their perception of you according to their experiences of you—on their beliefs and prejudices about you, on rumours about you and on the impression they have of you. You can't fully control it, so you need to put it out of your mind. Instead, it's essential to focus on the following: thinking in useful ways, which makes you smart; looking after yourself and being confident in yourself, which makes you attractive; being comfortable on your own, which makes you cool; doing what you do for a purpose and not giving up, which makes you successful; and practising what you do and being okay with mistakes, which makes you skilled.

Caring what other people think is a form of neediness, which is one of the most stupid, unattractive and uncool character traits. So go out today and start being okay with failing, being rejected and being in embarrassing situations. Learn to feel comfortable where you would have felt awkward, take yourself less seriously, quit over-analysing things and let yourself get lost in your experiences rather than being self-conscious all the time.

The more comfortable you are with these things, the more you will discover the freedom that comes with deciding 'Who cares what other people think?'

THE NATURE OF JEALOUSY

Jealousy is something that can break down relationships and become a dangerous obsession. In order to overcome another cause of the enemies of charisma, I want to talk about the nature of jealousy and, more importantly, of course, how to deal with it successfully.

When someone becomes jealous, they do so by thinking about what another person has, seems to have, or is. They then compare this with what they themselves have, and they feel inadequate. Although this generalisation is not always true, it certainly explains quite a lot of jealousy. Jealousy actually refers to a process. This process is the art of 'jealousising'. You see, what's crucial to remember is that when you think of things as the processes that they are, you develop control over them.

We 'jealousise' (yes, another word I made up—get over it) when we think of other people and compare ourselves with them. Jealousy manifests itself in a bad feeling, usually a mixture of longing, disappointment, frustration and inadequacy. It sometimes also leads people to engage in bad behaviour.

So there are a number of factors bound up with the nature of jealousy. In the modern world, many people seem to have been caught up in a constant search for fulfilment, in which nothing ever seems to be good enough. They see what others have and they want it, expecting that having it will make them satisfied. Instead, it simply creates a new desire for something else. For people like this, no matter what they do, they can't satisfy the craving, because the craving is a continuous strategy they run inside their head.

This can then become jealousy as they see others having what they imagine they want. Often they're annoyed by this and feel the need to downgrade the person they're jealous of, talking badly about them and attempting to put them in their place. This becomes jealousy manifested in begrudging or belittling. These are some suggestions as to the nature of jealousy. But what's the most effective way of dealing with it in yourself and in other people?

People who are not jealous focus instead on how well they themselves are doing, and they have a clever way of thinking about what they have and don't have. When they think of the things they want and that other people have, such as a wonderful relationship or career, or wealth, they remind themselves that it's almost certainly nowhere near as good in real life as it is in their imagination. They also remind themselves that they would have to give up certain things they take for granted in their own life in order to get those things.

They also learn from those who materially have what they want. They figure out the strategies that others used, they read books the others have read and they take the steps the others have taken. That way they focus their time on learning from those people instead of begrudging them. When doing this, it's important to remember the various options for comparing yourself with others. You can compare yourself with those you feel are better than you, which makes you feel bad; you can compare yourself with those you feel are worse than you, which will make you feel better; or you can do what's most useful, which is to compare yourself with you and ask, 'How much better are you doing?'

Jealousy can only exist if you become jealous. You can only become jealous if you think about other people having what you want and feel that that's somehow unfair. Sometimes people don't have what they deserve and sometimes they have more than they deserve. The key is to focus on improving your own life so you have what you want, regardless of who else has it or doesn't have it. It comes back to the old adage: live and let live.

When other people are jealous of you, the best way to deal with them is to remember that, no matter how much they begrudge you or insult you, it's a sign that you're succeeding. Every snipe, insult or criticism is most likely layered on top of a great desire to achieve what you've achieved or to be who you are. When you remember this, you'll feel a lot better.

As for relationships, if you've become jealous unnecessarily when your partner talks to other people, the key is to find out if you have a reason to worry about them being unfaithful. If you don't, become aware of the thoughts that make you feel bad when they're talking to other people. What kind of images do you make of them? Stop making images of him or her that make you feel bad and simply see the interactions for what they are: innocent conversation.

On the whole, jealousy can be dealt with by focusing on it as a process, developed from an attitude. It's essential to change your attitude, and once you do so, you will no longer be tortured by your own insecurities. Instead you will feel more secure in yourself and less needy. Learn to walk through the world as a learning machine, learning from others rather than envying them. Some people do seem to be lucky, but, in so many cases, you have to make yourself available for luck by making opportunities for yourself. What seems to be perfect never is when you have it, because perfection doesn't exist. That's why it's essential to feel more grateful for what you have in your life and appreciate all that's wonderful in every moment.

THE SEVEN ENEMIES OF CHARISMA

When you're comfortable with how other people think of you, and you've dealt successfully with any issues of jealousy that might exist, the next step is to defeat the fears of failure, rejection, embarrassment, seriousness, over-analysing, awkwardness and self-consciousness.

Now, the question is: how can you begin to do all this? Let's explore each enemy of charisma and discover how it's possible.

Fear of failure

When we first learn to walk, we don't fear failure. We're explorers, actively searching for success, and any attempt we make that's not successful is simply an activity that's not successful . . . yet! We continue to try different things until we succeed. We believe that, because another person can do it, it's possible for us to do so.

Then we grow up and begin to learn to notice our mistakes. Any time we're not successful we're made aware of it, and we're introduced to the notion of failure. Suddenly, not getting things right the first time is a big deal, and we put ourselves under pressure to master everything instantly. Whenever we didn't manage to succeed we learnt to consider it a failure, and we gave up with the excuse that we 'just weren't good enough' or that we were a 'failure'.

What's crucial to remember about all this is that just because we learnt these stupid ideas about failure it doesn't mean we have to be stuck with them. Instead, you can realise that there's another point of view you can have about failure. If you think about it, failure is almost inevitable with most tasks. It's how we learn to get better, to improve. The more you fail, the more information you have that can help you put things right.

Another important thing to remember is that failure often gets to people because they're striving for perfection. When they fail to do something perfectly they see their lack of success as a big deal. It's important to realise that if something were 'perfect', it could no longer improve. If it could no longer improve, there would be a limit to it, and anything that's limited can't be 'perfect'. The irony, therefore, is that nothing and no-one is perfect.

The key is not to be perfect or to get things right all the time but to be okay with losing and getting things wrong so that you can learn from your own mistakes, get out of your own way and do your very best the next time.

There are three ways to deal with a fear of failure.

1. Realise that there's no such thing as failure—only feedback. As long as you keep learning from your feedback and doing something different you can never fail.

2. Practise 'failing' as much as possible, and remember that every successful person has failed more than they have succeeded. Failure is necessary if you are to become successful. Children don't feel as if they've failed if they don't walk the first time they try: they keep going until they do. Remember, you miss 100 per cent of the shots you don't take.

3. If you don't get the result you wanted, instead of immediately asking yourself why, ask yourself, 'What do I need to do differently to get a successful result next time?' There's simply no point in thinking any other way.

Fear of rejection

We all have to deal with rejection. Our biggest problem is not that we get rejected but that we make such a big deal of it. Most people have a huge fear of rejection even when they haven't been rejected. They simply spend their time thinking of how bad they would feel if they were.

We can get rejected in lots of areas—from a job, from a social group or from a romantic interest. Now, although many people feel disappointed when they get rejected, the biggest problem is when people make disappointment out to be such a big deal.

One of the things you'll learn is that rejection is not about you: it's about the situation you're in. What we learn to do from an early age is to use all kinds of negative experiences and feedback in order to prove right the negative worries and thoughts we have about ourselves. We seem to put a big emphasis on being 'right'.

Instead, what's important is to realise and understand that when someone rejects us they do so knowing us only from certain limited experiences they have had, which are also distorted by their own limiting beliefs and learnt ways of thinking, up to that point. Their decision is not one made with all the information or based on all the facts: it's a decision based on many limited variables.

Knowing this, it's good to remember that the decision they make may be their mistake. The phrase 'It's their loss' may in fact have a lot of truth in it. Also, quite often people reject others because it's a wired-in response. In other words, it's something they're used to doing as a habit. For example, you're so used to rejecting door-to-door salespeople that you do so without a second thought, or you're so used to men coming on to you in a bar that your automatic response is to turn away.

So it's also essential to deal with rejection by looking at it as a potential automatic response that doesn't affect you in the slightest. When you see it as something that may be a mistake the other person is making, it's much easier to try again and change your approach slightly. That way you should wait for three unsuccessful attempts—at least—or until your gut is telling you it's a final answer before you give in.

There are four ways to deal with a fear of rejection.
1. Realise that it's not a rejection of you but of what the other person thinks they don't need or want at that moment.
2. Practise getting lots of rejections and make it so that it no longer bothers you. Remember, it's usually about what's going on for the

other person at that time that is the main reason for their rejecting you. If they do it nastily be pleased that you don't have to spend any more time with them again.

3. If you don't get the result you wanted, instead of asking why, immediately ask yourself, 'What do I need to do differently to get a successful result next time?' There's simply no point in thinking any other way.

4. Stop making pictures inside your head of what the other person is thinking and stop imagining yourself being rejected. Imagine these images small, far away and in black and white, and replace them with big, bright, colourful, close-up images of you being accepted and being brilliant.

Fear of embarrassment

The fear of embarrassment terrifies most people. Together with fears of failure and rejection, it's often the biggest cause of someone stopping themselves doing what they want to do. The thought of being embarrassed or, even worse, humiliated in front of other people is enough to prevent you talking to someone, asking someone out, saying something at a meeting or making a presentation.

What you have to realise about embarrassment is that it's only as big a deal as we make it. One of the things you will discover is that when you actually take a risk such as one of those just mentioned, you will find that even if you're embarrassed the experience of being embarrassed is nowhere near as bad as the feeling you had when you thought about what it would feel like.

You see, what happens is that we go inside our minds and make it out to be awful. When most people fear embarrassment, they do so by imagining everyone looking at them strangely. What's fascinating is that most of the time they don't even have specific people in mind who they imagine watching them. Often people ask, 'What will people think?' but it's very rare that they actually mention which people.

I remember having a couple of drinks with a friend, and I started to show her some exercise with your hands and face that improves the hemispherical connections between both parts of the brain. As I did it, however, she stopped me and said, 'People will start looking and thinking we're weird.' Looking around me and seeing only a handful of people, I asked her, 'Which people are you concerned about in particular?' She couldn't answer. As we looked around the room, searching for a person whose opinion she actually cared about, I asked her, 'Do you care what he thinks? Do you care what she thinks?' Eventually we got to the last person, and she realised that she actually didn't care what anyone else in that bar thought.

All too often we create this notion of 'people' and how we will be 'embarrassed' in front of 'them'. Think about the phrase 'I embarrassed myself', where 'embarrassing' is something you do to yourself. However, since embarrassment is a feeling, embarrassing yourself is not about actions: it's about how you create the feeling of embarrassment. Realistically, when you realise that you can only embarrass yourself if you feel embarrassed, you no longer ever need to feel that way.

There are four ways to deal with a fear of embarrassment.
1. Stop making images of what everybody must be thinking about you. Remember, most of them are too busy thinking about themselves.
2. Instead of asking, 'What are they thinking or looking at?' immediately inside your head repeat, 'So what? Who cares? How can I best present myself?'
3. Realise that embarrassment is created entirely inside your head and that if you decide not to be embarrassed you won't be.
4. Practise making a 'show' or a 'fool' of yourself and realise that the world doesn't come to an end. When you no longer care about that you can express yourself more wonderfully.

Finally, it's useful to learn how to create the states that are the opposite of these three fears (of failure, rejection and embarrassment). The examples above are my own. You will learn how to create these states later, in the chapter on turning yourself on (chapter 10).

Seriousness
When we take something seriously, we restrict our view of it and can only see it in a very rigid way. This means that we often feel quite bad when trying to tackle an issue, because we're focused on how 'serious' it is and on what critical implications it will have for our life, rather than on how we can deal with it. Seriousness makes us see something from only one point of view, and that's usually one with lots of negative feelings attached.

Consider how children learn so many things so rapidly when they're very young: they laugh, they play and they have fun. Then, as they go through the school system, they start taking things seriously, they get graded and they sit exams. Suddenly there's a huge drop in how quickly they can learn. Seriousness is actually a disease that can cripple a person's learning ability, as well as negatively affecting their success in communicating with others. As long as you take yourself seriously and care too much about what other people think, you will be stuck; but when you open up and begin to take things lightly you will find yourself free of the constraints of this limited mindset.

There are three main ways to deal with seriousness.
1. Whenever you face a challenging situation, ask yourself the question, 'How would a stand-up comedian describe this to their audience?'
2. Get lots of exposure to comedians, funny programmes and funny people. Make laughter a regular part of your life.
3. Every time you get serious, exaggerate your seriousness and laugh at yourself for being serious.

Over-analysing

When we over-analyse something, we get caught up in our own thoughts, which can affect our confidence. Often people have far too much time to think, and they spend that time talking to themselves in a negative way about their personality, their flaws, their relationships and their life. It's easy to criticise when you over-analyse anything, and it's also easy to make up ridiculous ideas and argue that they're true.

Over-analysing really restricts a person from being at their best socially, because it causes them to second-guess themselves at all times. Part of the experience of becoming a better communicator is being aware of how you come across and of how you can improve the way you do. That kind of analysis is fine and useful, but too much only serves to undermine confidence and discourage by negatively impacting on morale.

When you're free from over-analysing you will find it much easier to 'be yourself' and simply enjoy communicating with others. When you do that you often come across much better anyway.

There are three main ways to deal with over-analysing.
1. Get used to repeating this mantra inside your head: 'Shut up now, shut up now, shut up now.'
2. Focus on the outside world and pay more attention to the present moment than to going inside talking incessantly to yourself.
3. Whenever you ask yourself the questions 'Why?' or 'What if . . .?' unnecessarily, answer your own questions with 'Who cares?' and 'So what?'

Awkwardness
When we become awkward about something, it makes other people feel uncomfortable around us too.

Awkwardness is not something that exists 'in' a situation or 'between' two people: it's a state that we, together with the other person, create by the way we think. The more you create this feeling, the more it will be transmitted to the other person. This will result in you both feeling more and more uncomfortable and will prevent you from communicating at your very best.

When you learn to change the way you think, you realise that awkwardness is a choice and that you can choose to feel comfortable in all sorts of situations. This, in turn, will affect others around you, because when two people spend time together and are in opposing states, one feeling tends to dominate the other, and both people end up walking away with the same feeling. Therefore, feeling comfortable will help the other person to do that too, and this will make it easier for you to feel even more comfortable.

There are three main ways to deal with awkwardness.
1. Whenever you're talking to yourself about how awkward the situation is, repeat the mantra 'Shut up now, shut up now, shut up now.'
2. Remember, you can turn an awkward situation around by getting into a comfortable state that's stronger and longer-lasting than that of the other person or group. Eventually your feeling of comfort will win them over.
3. Stay on the outside and pay attention to the world. Most people feel awkward because they're too busy thinking to themselves.

It's useful to learn how to create the states that are the opposite of these three killers of success (seriousness, over-analysing and awkwardness). The examples above are my own. You will learn how to do this later.

Self-consciousness

The final enemy of charisma, self-consciousness, is related to some of the others. It involves being too focused on how you come across to other people. When people are self-conscious, they're so busy inside their own heads concentrating on everyone else's opinion that they don't perform effectively in whatever it is they're doing.

Take dancing, for example. If you go out to a nightclub and watch people dance, you will realise that the best dancers are the ones who are lost in the music. They don't seem to care about what other people think. They're too busy enjoying themselves and letting themselves be moved by the music. That's the key. The more you allow yourself to become lost in whatever activity you're doing, the more you will discover how to completely eliminate self-consciousness.

Now, when I talk about becoming lost in the experience, I mean doing the experience as effectively as possible and enjoying the process. For example, if you're giving a presentation, you allow yourself to present as effectively as possible while paying attention to the feedback from the audience. However, you're not concerned with what the audience thinks about you. You're so involved in the presentation that your only concern regarding the audience is that they're learning and getting from it what you want and need them to be getting.

There are three main ways to deal with self-consciousness.

1. Pay attention to whatever activity you're doing or whatever conversation you're in. Focusing on how you feel is a sure way of becoming self-conscious. Instead, focus on losing yourself in each moment.

2. Stop over-analysing and stop doing too much self-examination. This can be useful up to a point, but when it no longer is repeat the mantra 'Shut up now, shut up now, shut up now.'

3. Get into more useful states, such as being more playful, aware and centred. You can learn how to do this in chapter 10.

Chapter 9
The physiology of charisma

You do not run from a bear because you are afraid of it, but rather become afraid of the bear because you run from it.

WILLIAM JAMES

One of the things I learnt very early on in my battle with depression was the importance of how I moved my body whenever I was feeling bad. I noticed that when I forced myself to get out of the posture I was in when I was experiencing a real low, it helped. You know, it's far, far easier to be depressed when you're lying down or curled up than it is when you're standing tall or walking briskly somewhere.

Every person carries around with them a source of many 'illegal' drugs in their brain. Our brains are full of chemicals that create very powerful results in our bodies. In fact, often when a person takes drugs, it's not the drugs themselves that have the effect on them but their body's response to it. When you take a drug, it binds to receptors in your brain, and they react by releasing particular neurotransmitters that correspond to the specific feeling.

Once you understand this, the good news is that you have control over the chemistry in your brain. This chemistry is fundamentally different when you're feeling shy from when you're feeling confident. What I want to explain to you in this chapter is how you can gain more control over the chemistry in your brain and understand more about how it works, so that you can create chemicals that affect you positively and that affect everyone you meet in the same way.

Your brain is made up of millions of tiny nerve cells called neurons. These are connected by firing electrical and chemical impulses to each other back and forth across bridge-like structures called synapses. Your brain is constantly sending messages and signals between millions of neurons. These messages are both electrical and chemical.

Whenever you feel good and are in a good state, your brain responds by chemically releasing neurotransmitters such as serotonin and dopamine. This gives you a good feeling, and your brain chemistry is thereby working well. The better your brain chemistry is working, the more effectively you're able to use it. Therefore the state you're in is extremely important not only for the feeling that you enjoy but also because it means that you will be literally working better.

THE NEUROCHEMISTRY OF POSTURE

Of all the various things I've learned from the field of NLP, the impact of your body's posture on how you feel ranks up there. A fascinating study was conducted by the Harvard professor Amy Cuddy and her colleagues that revealed exciting facts about body language and, in particular, the impact it has on our brains and neurochemistry. They split forty-two male and female participants into two groups. One group were encouraged to get into two powerful poses back to back. One of these, for example, was the 'hands behind head and feet on the desk' pose. The other group were to get into two restrictive poses, for example clamping their arms, hands and legs shut. After two minutes, the saliva of both groups was analysed and compared with a sample taken beforehand.

Even in this short time, the power group's saliva showed a significant increase in the hormone testosterone (associated with power and confidence) and a decrease in cortisol (associated with stress and anxiety), while the restricted group showed the opposite. This fascinating result revealed that simply altering your posture can have an immediate effect on your neurochemistry.

Physiology refers to how we hold our body. It considers whether or not your head is held up, whether or not you're smiling, how you're walking, what your posture is like—in short, how your body is positioned and moving. There's a certain physiology attached to personal charisma.

You can literally alter the way you feel by how you use your body.

When you use your body in a certain way it will help you change your state. Now, although many people 'get this', most don't realise what it means: that every single physical action you already take when you're feeling good is a powerful way to immediately make you feel that way.

Take breathing, for example. When most people are told about breathing to relax they often learn a complicated method. They learn to do it in a very specific way. Instead, remember a time when you were really exhausted and you breathed a big sigh of relief that the day was over. Remember the breath you took as you fell onto the bed, got into a warm bath or sank into a chair at home. That sigh is the sigh you use naturally to get yourself into a very relaxed state. Try it now. Take a deep breath and really sigh, letting your entire body go as you do this. You'll notice yourself immediately feeling really, really relaxed.

The fact is that the breath itself actually relaxed you the way you wanted it to and made you feel immediately relieved. In this way, the physiology of your body creates a set of conditions for you to feel certain kinds of feeling.

Therefore by learning to control your physiology you can continually create the optimum condition for you to feel how you want to feel. A good way to get out of the state you're in, for example, is to pay attention to your posture, breathing, movement and so on. Then shake yourself out completely, move your body into the completely opposite physiology and notice how differently you feel.

Every emotion, every feeling has a specific way of breathing associated with it and a specific posture and pattern of movement. When you notice this, you can deliberately change your breathing, posture and movement, and you will find that your feelings change. More importantly for us, when you start breathing differently and positioning and moving your body in new ways that reflect confidence, comfort and expressiveness you will start to feel those feelings too.

What's also crucial to know is that the stress and tension in your body has an impact on your thinking process. Your body controls the flow of communication that goes in and out through you. By this, I mean simply that the flexibility of your physiology will have a significant effect on your ability to take in information and to express it clearly and smoothly. That's one of the reasons why stretching and exercising is good not only for your well-being and health but also for your state of mind.

THE 'POSTURE OF EXCELLENCE' EXERCISE

Practise walking, standing and sitting in a more confident way. You will notice when you change your physiology that you will feel differently as a result.

Chapter 10
How to turn yourself on

Always act like you're wearing an invisible crown.

ANON.

In the early 1970s, Richard Bandler and John Grinder of the University of California, Santa Cruz, teamed up to study the most successful therapists at that time. They explored the work of Fritz Perls, Virginia Satir and Milton H. Erickson, all of whom had built an impressive following, despite using different forms of therapy. They examined how these therapists thought and acted and what skills they used in getting such great results. What they discovered from this process, known as 'modelling', was that there was a systematic structure in what these therapists did to help their clients make changes.

Bandler and Grinder continued to apply their methodology and found it working just as well when they mapped the most successful people in a number of other areas. Neuro-linguistic programming (NLP) was the name they gave to their attitude and methodology.

I've been involved in NLP since I first read a book about it when I was only fourteen. It's one of the most important tools for personal development I've ever used. Richard soon became a mentor to me, and we've since collaborated on a number of books. Although the field of NLP is vast, one of the essential lessons he used to repeat to me over and over again was that of the importance of state. He used to constantly remind me to focus on first going into whatever state I wanted the client to be in, until it became second nature to me.

In order to do that, I learnt a number of strategies for accessing the most resourceful states possible. Here, I'd like to take you step by step through how you can create the kind of feelings you want, whenever you want them.

Creating internal states is all about using your imagination in particular ways. There are two keys to creating states. Firstly, you must learn how to create certain feelings by using your imagination. Secondly, you must learn how to capture those feelings and trigger them whenever you need to in your life.

THE CREATION OF A STATE

A state is created when a person's brain chemistry is activated. It may be activated by the circumstances they're experiencing and the effect this has on their brain, or, crucially, it may be activated by the thoughts they're having and the effect this has on their brain.

For example, think about a particular activity you enjoy. When you're enjoying that activity you naturally seem to go into positive and happy states. Take laughing: whenever you're laughing you immediately create positive chemicals in your brain and you feel good. Thus, by laughing, you affect your state.

Now, have you ever had an experience where you remembered something that once made you laugh and, even though it was no longer happening, you laughed again? This is an example of how, simply by using your memory, you're able to regain access to the good feelings attached to them.

The nervous system can't tell the difference between a real and a vividly imagined experience. So when you want to create feelings inside yourself, you can simply imagine experiences where you felt the same feelings. If you do it vividly enough, the feelings will return.

You can also create such positive feelings by imagining how good you will feel in the future. Any time you're excited about something it's because you're thinking about what you'll be feeling when you experience it. The anticipation of this good feeling is called excitement, which is created entirely inside your own head.

The great news is that every state is affected by what you do inside your head. The key is to learn how you can control, change and affect this. Once you learn this it gives you the ability to change the state you're in by diminishing negative states and increasing positive and useful ones.

Now, so far, you've learnt that by changing your physiology you can change your state. There's another approach that involves changing how you think. Every state is made of certain kinds of thoughts. Basically, when we think, we all make pictures and images, talk to ourselves, hear internal sounds and have internal feelings, tastes and smells. Our thoughts are constructed through these sensory channels or modalities.

The specific qualities of each modality are known as 'submodalities'. These are the building blocks of our internal world. Just as a television has brightness, colour and volume controls, so our brains have their own controls, which determine what we feel and how intensely we feel it.

Consider what it would be like to know how to run your own brain. What will be possible when you discover how to control how you experience the world more effectively? How does this enable you to build more powerful states in yourself and others? Simply by changing the submodalities of a thought or sequence of thoughts, you can dramatically enhance how powerful that thought feels.

For example, imagine seeing yourself at a time when you felt really good. See a small black-and-white image, a still image. Notice the feeling. Now imagine stepping inside the image as it becomes huge, bigger than a cinema screen. Make it really colourful. Imagine seeing through your eyes, hearing through your ears and feeling the feelings as you experience this time again. Make things brighter and bigger— notice the feeling.

What you'll find is that the new experience feels much more intense than the previous one. That's because you're telling your brain to think differently about these situations. You're teaching it to give you a burst of feelings similar to those you had back then.

Similarly, take a person you don't like or who has made you feel bad or some other kind of negative feeling. Figure out how you represent the negative image of them and make it go further away, smaller, dimmer. Slow it down, make it black and white and turn it into a still image. You can imagine a clown's nose on a person who once made you feel bad. You can take your negative inner voice, change its tone and make it ridiculous, like Mickey Mouse. You can take your feelings and imagine them going through your body in the opposite direction.

With this awareness of submodalities, play around with what happens when you change each one. If you're watching yourself in the experience, imagine what it would be like to be in it. If you're talking to yourself in a positive tone of voice, find out what happens when you make it even more positive and strong. If you're feeling the good feeling first in your chest, imagine it going through all parts of your body. Play around and notice what happens. What you will find is that, as you do, you will find yourself feeling that feeling more intensely or less intensely depending on what you do.

By being aware of submodalities, you will discover how to intensify states powerfully, get rid of negative feelings and understand more accurately how others are thinking. Usually when people imagine themselves in the experience and imagine it like a film—in colour, big and bright and close—and hear the sound surrounding them and hear themselves talking to themselves positively and powerfully, feeling the feelings spreading around their body, it makes the feelings more intense.

So, really, the method for creating a powerful, positive state is:

1. Imagine who you would be at your best or who you have been at your best.
2. See a film of yourself being really confident in a charismatic way. Make it really vivid and real. Change the submodalities so the image is crystal clear and vividly strong.
3. Step into the film and see through those eyes, hear through those ears, feel through those feelings. Run through the entire film and let yourself feel all the feelings filling you.

THE TRIGGERS OF A STATE

Every time a successful athlete goes to perform, they engage in certain mental acts to 'psych themselves up'. Often we engage in a different kind of mental act: we 'psych ourselves out'. What this means is that we think in ways that make us perform worse, not better.

That's one major lesson we can learn from athletes. They make themselves perform better by using certain triggers that enable them to get into the right state as quickly as possible. For example, the love of my life, Glasgow Celtic, do the famous 'huddle' before a football match as a ritual that gets them into that state. The great All Blacks in rugby do the haka, which has the same kind of effect.

These triggers are particular things you can do or actions you can take that need to be linked to specific states. Once you've linked them, when you use such actions again they will trigger the specific states you've linked them to. For example, you might have a phobia about spiders because one day you linked the feeling of terror with the object 'spider'. You created for yourself a negative trigger of fear and attached it to the spider (these triggers are also called 'anchors').

But as well as triggers or anchors that create negative states in an instant, there are also examples of anchors that create positive states in an instant. For example, a particular song on the radio can sometimes bring you to a state of love, as it reminds you of an experience of feeling that way. What I'm looking at here are the triggers you can set up deliberately and use.

Anchoring enables you to capture and regain access to positive experiences and feelings to use more powerfully later on. Anchors re-induce emotional states and are used widely throughout the world, from everyday conversation right through to advertisements. Most sales are basically a result of anchoring a good feeling to a product or service.

Another example is 'that look' you get when you know you're in trouble. Although all you see is someone squinting or twitching their facial muscles, you immediately begin to feel the anticipation of a negative interaction. You've associated this face with a negative feeling.

Anchors are everywhere. There are visual anchors (things you see that induce certain states), auditory anchors (things you hear that induce them) and anchors that are kinaesthetic (things you feel), olfactory (smell) and gustatory (taste).

For example, an image of a beautiful model is often used in television advertisements to create the state of lust, which the advertisers then link to their product. Most lovers have a particular song that brings them into a wonderful state of love, as it was played during a significant time in their relationship. The smell of freshly cut grass is often an anchor that gives people feelings of youth and aliveness. The taste of certain sweets might induce a particular state that we haven't been in for years. Kissing is a form of kinaesthetic anchoring that involves a particular touch, creating a powerful feeling in the person. Although I'd like to point out that kissing is really only wet tissue causing friction off wet tissue (yes, I know, I'm a real romantic!), most of the good feelings that come with kissing derive from our associations with it. Since these anchors exist, it's important to learn how to create the most useful anchors. Imagine if you could feel how you want to feel, when you want to.

Next, we will explore the different states that you would want to anchor to become more charismatic. Once we have decided this, there's a very powerful technique known as 'charisma squared' that will teach you to anchor these states powerfully.

THE UNITED STATES OF CHARISMA

Having completed exhaustive research into the components of the kinds of emotional states the most charismatic individuals go into, I've found four main states that I call the four Ps: power, passion, present and playful.

These emotional states are the fundamental essence of charisma from a 'being' point of view. When you go into these states you will find yourself emanating a charismatic impression to others simply by how you feel.

It makes complete sense that these states are so powerful. If you think about it, what you've already learnt is that your state has a significant impact on those you communicate with. So, since states are contagious, when you feel these states so will your audience. And you want them to.

You want them to feel powerful, confident and certain in you as a communicator. When you feel sure of yourself, so will they. You want them to feel passionate about what you're telling them. You feel excited—so will they. You want to be completely present with them. You feel calm and attentive, and so will they. You want them to feel playful. If you're enjoying yourself, so will they. This is incredibly powerful and useful knowledge.

By going into these states you guarantee that, even without words, you start generating the kind of feelings you want in the people you're communicating with.

Power: A state of confidence and certainty in yourself and what you're saying.

Passion: A state of energy and excitement about what you're saying and your purpose.

Presence: A state of being centred on and composed by being in the moment and fully attentive to your surroundings.

Playfulness: A state of being fun to be with and enjoying yourself with others.

So, how do you create these four states and anchor them so you can create them in an instant?

THE 'CHARISMA SQUARED' TECHNIQUE

1. Think of a situation where you would like to feel and act charismatically.

2. Choose the states (power, passion, presence and playfulness) you'd like to be feeling in that situation.

3. Stand up and visualise a square in your favourite colour on the ground in front of you. Next, visualise yourself standing in that square, filled with your favourite colour in the state of power. See how you'd look at your most powerful. Notice the smile on your face, your posture, the way you stand.

4. Once you've visualised that self vividly, step into your imaginary self in the square.

5. See what you'd see, hear what you'd hear, feel what you'd feel, and imagine the feeling of power filling you up as you take a deep breath. Imagine that the colour of the square gets stronger and feel it immerse you.

6. After experiencing this wonderful feeling for a few moments, step out of the square and think of something else.

7. Repeat steps 3–6, each time adding the next state. So, next time with power and passion; then power, passion and presence; and finally power, passion, presence and playfulness.

8. Imagine yourself in a situation where you want to be more charismatic. Imagine yourself going through it and step into your square. Notice how much better you feel, and go through the same experience with the new feelings of being charismatic.

9. Mastery over your feelings, thoughts and attitude is a crucial first step, but to become more charismatic—to get the charismatic edge—you also need to align your behaviours with your attitude. You need to know the actions of charisma.

Part 2

Step forward: The actions of charisma

A barking dog is often more useful than a sleeping lion.

WASHINGTON IRVING

A few years ago, I cracked two discs in the back of my neck. The discs pinched down on a nerve, and what I experienced was the most agonising physical pain I've ever faced. It was torture. The result of a mixture of hundreds of flights on my travels around the world and motorbike crashes in Thailand and Nicaragua, it meant that my past finally caught up with me. As ever, I kept asking questions about what I needed to do in order to get stronger and fix the problem. I was taught a number of key behavioural changes I needed to make to strengthen my neck.

I had to walk differently, sit differently, stand differently. I had to read in a different posture and use the computer differently. But it needed to be done. So I did it. I practised these new behaviours over and over again until they became automatic. Now, a few years on, I'm in great condition, and my neck, with some regular care, is a lot better than it was. This was only possible because I implemented new behaviours and made them habits.

Having successfully worked on your attitude, you now need to build consistent habits or new behaviours into your life. To be charismatic, you need to make sure you create the kind of impression you want in the minds of other people. Most of the following advice didn't come naturally to me. Instead, I worked on every suggestion over and over again. I fundamentally believe that if you want to succeed in this life you need to do whatever it takes to ensure that you're doing all you can.

Charles Duhigg, author of *The Power of Habit*, suggests that building useful habits is one of the most important things you can do for yourself. In his enlightening book, he argues that building a habit is a simple process: there's a cue for a certain behaviour, followed by a routine, followed by a reward. You can change a habit by figuring out a new habit to replace it with that will lead to the same reward afterwards.

So, again, there's a cue, at which point you practise a new behaviour and then follow it with the same reward. If you want to stop smoking, for example, and your cue is stress and the reward is relaxation, you simply find another routine that you can practise whenever you get stressed (such as a breathing technique) that leads you to the reward of relaxation, and you practise it whenever you find yourself in that situation in the future.

Duhigg also explains the importance of creating habits. The idea is that we have far too many decisions to make in our lives, and it can be exhausting. But when you begin to create habit after habit, you find yourself automatically doing a lot of new behaviours effectively and so saving your energy.

What do we mean by habits in this case? Well, once you've built a strong internal sense of charisma, the next dimension to work on is how to present yourself to the world. Being happy with yourself and feeling confident in what you can do is important. The next step, however, is to make sure that the way you feel inside about yourself becomes the way others feel inside about you too. It's about learning to position and present yourself through what you do, in the most useful way possible.

A few years ago I worked on the television programme 'Ask Anna' with a great guy called Bryan, who was looking for help from the presenter, Anna Nolan, about how to get on better with women. Bryan's problem was that, although he was confident, he wasn't creating the right kind of impression in the minds of the women he dated. So, as part of the programme, the first thing we did was to organise three dates with three different women and record them on video so we could analyse them.

After the dates, all three women said Bryan was a lovely guy. He was smart, friendly and fun, and they all felt he would make a perfect best friend. Confidence wasn't a big issue for Bryan, but his problem was that he was coming across in a way that wasn't enticing or attractive to them. After I sat down with Bryan and watched the analysis and comments, I explained to him that, although he had a massive amount going for him and was a terrific catch, the challenge was that he had a habit in how he communicated of seeming more feminine than he might have intended. When I suggested this, Anna asked if I was trying to argue that he should change who he was. I responded that, of course, Bryan was fine the way he was, inside. The problem was the impression he was creating.

Every time you meet someone, they begin a process of evaluating you in certain ways, according to how you're dressed, your posture, your voice, your words, the way you move, your emotional state, how you react to a situation and so on. They analyse you automatically and come to certain conclusions about you. In fact, we all do it. I'm often asked, as a psychologist, whether or not I spend a lot of time analysing other people when I first meet them. Although people are afraid of me doing that, the reality is that we all do it, instinctively and automatically. We're constantly making decisions about those we meet.

What this means is that you need to be aware of how you're coming across to other people, and you also need to be in a position where you're far more aware of other people. The skills of presenting a great impression of yourself and of reading others are critical to you being a more engaging and charismatic communicator.

So I explained to Bryan and Anna that he was fantastic the way he was as a person but that he needed to make some changes to his behaviour in order to come across in a more attractive way. From the way he was drinking and eating to certain mannerisms, there were a few small shifts in behaviour that could make a big difference. By helping Bryan to adjust so that he was drinking and eating in a more masculine way, it actually helped him tap into his masculine side and made him more attractive to the opposite sex. In fact, at the end of the programme, at a dinner party where Bryan and two other single men met three single women, he had all three women interested in dating him. It was his simple adjustment of behaviour that made the big difference.

Of course, being authentic is absolutely critical to being truly charismatic. The key is to know that you will still have to behave differently with different people. You don't behave the same way with your mother as with your wife, or with your husband as with your son. You change how you relate to them and communicate with them depending on the role you play and what the interaction calls for.

In a frequently quoted study on charisma conducted in 1989, two researchers, J. M. Howell and P. J. Frost, taught various 'charisma behaviours' to actors to see if it would help them be perceived by others as being more charismatic. These included 'extended eye contact, vocal variety and using animated facial expression'. They were given the same script as other actors who were to make no such non-verbal changes, but they were perceived by the subjects in the experiment as possessing much more charisma. So, putting on the behaviour showed a marked improvement in how charismatic you seemed to be.

According to tradition, we have five senses through which we perceive the world and, indeed, how we perceive other people in it. We see, hear, touch, smell and taste. So it's important when you're attempting to come across more charismatically that you use these senses, in particular that you look, sound and feel more charismatic. (Smelling and tasting more charismatic isn't something I'm going to spend much more time on in this book, for obvious reasons . . . especially taste!)

In this part of the book, I want to explain what I've discovered to be some of the essential steps towards communicating and relating to others in such a way as to create the most engaging and enticing impression possible. What are the most important practical behavioural changes you can make, immediately, to come across in a more charismatic way? What do the best communicators do differently? How do you create the best kind of impression when you first meet someone? What are the steps you need to take in order to read people and understand them better? How can you get on with anyone, quickly and easily? How do you need to dress, speak, walk and talk to be perceived by others as possessing presence and charisma? Here I want to share with you the behavioural keys to stepping forward into the most attractive and appealing you.

Chapter 11
The twelve habits of great communicators

When the mouse laughs at the cat, there is a hole nearby.

NIGERIAN PROVERB

Two experts in the area of willpower, Roy F. Baumeister and John Tierney, suggest that it is indeed possible to train people to have better willpower. Since willpower is regarded by many as one of the most important qualities to have in order to improve your life, this discovery is potentially game-changing.

The idea that willpower can be trained and improved at first seemed to contradict what the research had so far suggested. By means of a number of what were known as 'ego-depletion experiments', researchers found that when people expended time resisting temptation in one area they found themselves lacking willpower in another. So it suggested that our willpower can be depleted when we use it in one area of our lives.

What Baumeister and Tierney suggest is that if you make adjustments to a number of different areas of your life, and if you practise disciplining yourself in these new areas, the knock-on effect for your other behaviours will be that you'll find yourself having a greater resource of willpower at your disposal. You'll find yourself being able to draw upon a bigger and bigger pool of power when you need it. So if you want to stop smoking, make a number of other positive changes and you'll find yourself stronger and better able to do so.

To start building more charismatic behaviours and actions into your daily life it's probably the best idea to practise making a number of positive changes at once and to get yourself into the right frame of mind for building your own discipline. Habits are built this way, and once you build a habit you no longer even need willpower for that behaviour.

You see, Baumeister and Tierney argue that, in making decisions all day long, you're also depleting your ego, and you can therefore experience a kind of decision fatigue. When this happens you're not only more susceptible to temptation but often more likely to find yourself in a negative state and not necessarily making the smartest or fairest decisions. The implications of this are that building habits and creating routines can enable you to perform daily much more effectively and productively. Instead of having to motivate yourself to engage in positive behaviours, you make them habits so that they happen automatically when you most need them to.

Indeed, Barack Obama, in the interview quoted in chapter 7, has explained how he does this. As the 'decider'—as George W. Bush referred to the job of president—Obama has said he always makes sure to make as few personal decisions every day as possible, because he has so many professional decisions to make. He explains:

> You'll see I wear only gray or blue suits. I'm trying to pare down decisions. I don't want to make decisions about what I'm eating or wearing. Because I have too many other decisions to make . . . you need to focus your decision-making energy. You need to routinise yourself.

So it's critical that you begin to value creating habits in how you communicate that allow you to act naturally and automatically. This ensures that you're performing more efficiently, far more of the time. It allows you to know that your default state is that of a great communicator.

There are some things the best communicators know that most people don't, some things they do that most people don't. A colleague of mine, Alessio Roberti, often presents a wonderful workshop session analysing one of Steve Jobs's speeches. In it, Alessio breaks down almost every move that Jobs makes and explains how much thought actually went into the presentation. Everything Jobs does, everything he says, everywhere he moves—it's all choreographed perfectly. Alessio can spend an entire hour on five minutes of footage, and it's a fascinating hour!

The reason it's so fascinating is the same reason that NLP is so fascinating: it offers you a real insight into how the most successful communicators think and behave. It explains how they use language and win over their audience powerfully. Whenever I teach people about world-class communicators, a lot of the magic is in the details. The apparent spontaneity is far from that. There's a massive amount of time and a massive amount of hard work put into becoming truly exceptional at getting a message across. You could spend years learning the finest distinctions and refining your technique. It's a huge field.

But at the core of what the very best do are a number of patterns that you can see repeated over and over again. If charisma is an impression you create in the mind of another person, one of the absolutely critical things, on top of having a certain attitude towards yourself, is your ability to affect other people.

As I discussed earlier, if you attempt merely to change your outward behaviour and neglect your inner world you will be faking that behaviour, and people will know. To truly be a more powerful communicator, change must move from the inside out. However, once you've altered your attitude you then need to take the right kind of actions in order for you to come across in the best possible way.

So in this chapter the best place to start is to examine what the very best communicators in the world do when they interact with others. I've identified twelve habits that tend to be replicated by the best communicators.

1. Remember them, not just their name

Bill Clinton was famous for making anyone he spoke to feel like the only person in the room. He would lock in his gaze and give them 100 per cent of his attention, and that captivated them. But what really made the difference was that this wasn't just a 'communication trick': Bill really did pay attention to them. Not only did he remember people's names really well but he would also remember the names of their children. He would 'know' them, and that generated a sense of him being a good, caring person.

In reality, the best communicators I've ever met don't just remember names: they remember people. They might remember your dog's breed, the age of your children, the colour of your car; but they will remember enough to convince you that you matter to them.

When people demonstrate that they remember you and something about your life, you feel like they see you as the unique person you are. That matters. In this world, where communication is faster and more superficial than ever before, someone who goes a little deeper can make far more of an impact.

In order to remember that person, get into the habit of actually visualising their life as they describe it. As they tell you about their dog, for example, imagine the dog running about with them at their home. By making what they say into a vivid visualisation, you're far more likely to remember it.

2. Show that you care

Although he's an example of a horrendous human being, Adolf Hitler was extremely influential, largely for one reason: his passion. If you ever get a chance to see footage of him speaking you will see that he rants and raves a lot. He always looks angry, which most people would assume is not a good state to be in when communicating. The reality, though, is that he genuinely looks as if things really bother him. Because he was talking about the kind of things that many people in Germany were angry about, he resonated with them.

Showing that you care about your message or cause makes other people feel like they need to pay attention to it. It ups the ante of the conversation and makes every word that much more important. When you care about your subject, other people will too, and they will be moved by you—even if you're a psychopath like Hitler. (Obviously I'm assuming that, since you had the good taste to buy this book, this is not true of you!)

The best way to show you care is to really connect with the reasons you care so much and to remember that your job is to help other people care as much as you. You need to consider what's so important about what you have to say, and why people need to listen. When you're focused on that you will find yourself feeling a strong sense of passion for what you're talking about. It's also a good idea to be more expressive when you talk to others. People need to feel that your words match your voice and your gestures.

3. Demonstrate competence

In a study on charisma conducted on a mixture of Americans and Koreans in 2005, two researchers, Yeon Choi and Jeongkoo Yoon, found that the participants felt that the perception of competence significantly increased how charismatic someone was perceived to be. So when you demonstrate that you can do something well it automatically makes you seem more charismatic. You could almost explain this as an example of what could be called 'performance charisma' connected to what a person does really well.

People are very interested in meeting Tiger Woods, for example, because of what he's achieved. It doesn't necessarily mean that he's charismatic. Yet he does have an impact because of the impression he creates in the mind of other people. So, in a way, his status or performance enables him to come across in a charismatic way.

Obviously, the best thing to do to make this a habit is to become better at whatever you're doing. But from a skill-based point of view, if you become really competent at speaking, communicating, influencing, joking and telling stories, people will perceive you as being more charismatic as a result.

4. Get into their shoes

When I attended Harvard Business School and studied strategic negotiation, I was lucky enough to spend a lot of time with some world-class negotiators. They discussed a number of strategies they employ in every billion-dollar negotiation they're involved in. Probably one of the most important strategies was what they did before an actual meeting. Instead of focusing on what they were going to do at the table, the very best focused on what they would do before they got to it.

They would sit down and plot out the various stakeholders at the meeting and ask themselves the following question: What's in this deal for each stakeholder? They would be very careful to meticulously plan and prepare for all sorts of goals, values, reactions and responses from each person at the table. Getting into someone else's shoes is critical.

You know what they say about getting into another person's shoes? Walk a mile in their shoes and . . . you'll have their shoes—and you'll be a mile away! In reality, though, the perspective of the other person must always be considered carefully when communicating. Remember, they have their ego, and you can either positively affect it or negatively effect it. People remember being given attention, approval, compliments, congratulations, validation and recognition.

Always ensure that you do this with those you communicate with when it's useful. Also ensure that you use plenty of tact and diplomacy when talking with people. Pay attention to all the information you're getting and demonstrate respect for others, regardless of their position or status.

Always ask yourself, 'What does the other person need or want?' and 'How can I help them get that?'—as long as it's useful and good for you too. Consider how you come across to others. Imagine being in their shoes and seeing, hearing and experiencing yourself. Ask yourself what changes you need to make. This will help you gain more self-insight.

5. Start the ball rolling

Have you ever been in a situation where, before you were about to meet someone, you weren't sure about how to greet them? Maybe you had a number of choices: a nod, a handshake, a bow, a hug, a kiss on one cheek, a kiss on both cheeks? Such an array of choices can make the first few seconds of a meeting seem like a huge challenge. I've often found myself in this situation, creating instant embarrassment from the get-go simply because I allowed such uncertainty to exist.

The first step is to give your best guess according to the situation, context and background of the person to determine what's appropriate. You need to consider their religion, where they're from, how well you know them and what kind of person they might be. The next step is that, once you decide, it's a good idea to initiate the handshake or hug or kiss reciprocation so that there's no time for any awkwardness for those first few seconds.

In a number of well-known companies, part of the recruitment process is a session in which they bring together all the applicants for a leadership position and simply observe their interactions. One of the things they watch for is who tends to take charge of the context in an unfamiliar setting. It's easy to spot strong leaders emerging when you see them introducing themselves to others and starting the conversation. Getting the ball rolling is a sign not only of leadership but of someone who's very comfortable with themselves and others.

Most of the time, people get nervous because of the uncertainty of such situations. The context may be unfamiliar or there isn't an obvious and clear set of guidelines on how people should act with each other. Once you figure out the best way to act, get used to walking straight up to people and introducing yourself. This projects you as confident, easy to talk to and friendly. Do all you can to appear approachable, making it easy for the other person in a conversation.

This is a good idea not only from the point of view of an actual first impression, or even from the point of view of a social lubricant: getting into the habit of approaching people instantly helps you get out of your head and avoid over-analysing what's going on. Since over-analysis can lead to self-consciousness, thinking less can actually help you to do far better.

6. Pay attention to everyone

Being strategic in communication means thinking not just about what you say but about what other people will say about what you've said. It's really important to remember that the people who matter aren't just the people who matter but the ones who matter to the people who matter. In other words, always make sure you create the impression you want in all the people you meet, not just those you want to influence. If you're trying to impress a romantic interest, make sure that you're really nice to their friends, as how their friends perceive you will influence that person's perception of you.

The impression you create in the mind of another person continually adjusts after you've gone. The best way to control it is to make sure that you've paid good attention to the other people in a situation. When other people are around, think about any meeting you have with one person as a meeting with all those people. You might focus on the key stakeholder, but remember that their friends or colleagues may well be reading you as well.

Look around at everyone and make eye contact with them as you communicate. Always be aware of what you notice in your peripheral vision and keep an eye out for two members of the group looking at each other or smiling. There may well be hidden conversations going on, and it's good for you to be aware of that so you can pay special attention to bringing them out of their smirking exchange to engage with you.

7. Questions are the answer

Asking questions is a wonderful way of finding out more information about the other person and, at the same time, of making them feel like you value them and their lives. When you ask questions you show interest in them, and you also find out valuable information that can be useful.

Questions direct the attention of the person. So if you want someone to feel a certain way you can use questions that induce that state. For example, if you wanted a customer to feel good about buying a particular product, you might ask them about a product they have bought in the past that they were really happy with. As they describe the product they will experience again that same emotion and therefore be in a more receptive state to buy.

Paul Newman once said of Bill Clinton after they went to dinner together that 'it's nice to have a president adept at the fine art of listening.' Indeed, the ability to listen and take in what others are saying gives you a real edge over everyone else. Most people hear, but few really listen.

8. Give genuine praise

In my work with Bryan (as discussed in part 2) one of the other things I did to help him with women was to change how he thought about, and therefore performed, the act of flirting. We went into a pub one evening and I gave him a challenge. One exercise I brought him through worked like this.

What he had to do was to go to the bar, buy a couple of drinks for us and, on his way back, approach a woman he found attractive and deliver a one-line compliment. It had to be something he really did find attractive about her. The way he had to say it was this: 'Excuse me, sorry for interrupting. I can't stay, but I just had to come over and say . . .' The twist was this: immediately after he did this, he had to return to me and not talk to the woman again . . . ever!

Now, this seemed counterintuitive. Complimenting a woman seems like it should lead to her feeling good and to you staying around. But this is the wrong way to see compliments. Many people use compliments as a 'technique' to influence a person. They try and use the compliment to get what they want from them. Whether it's an example of arse-kissing in business, of trying to have your friend like you more or of trying to seduce someone, it's the same game.

But compliments given with this attitude never have the desired effect, because people can feel when you're doing something in order to get something and when you're doing it for the right reasons. The trick is to learn to compliment for one reason alone: to make the other person feel really good. You see, when Bryan knew he had to walk away after delivering the compliment it made sure that what he said was said for the right reason. Since he wasn't looking for anything, he said what he did to make them feel good about themselves. He wasn't looking for anything in return, and they felt that. The funny part was that each time he did it the woman would keep looking over at him.

Sometimes the problem isn't what we do but why we do it. When you change the 'why', you can change the way they react to you. Of course, people like when you tell them they're great—but only when they believe you're being genuine. Ask yourself the question, 'What do I like about this person?' Then you'll find the answer. It may take you a little longer for some people, but you'll always find something in everyone, and complimenting them about this can really help you to connect with them more deeply.

9. Ask for help

Many people are under the impression that when you do a favour for someone, it causes them to like you more. Now, this may well be true. What fewer people know is that asking someone for help actually makes them like you more, because when they actually do whatever they do for you they're forced to justify to themselves why they're doing it and why they're taking the time to help you. This commitment of time is then usually interpreted as being done because they must 'like' you.

Cognitive dissonance refers to the state of holding two conflicting views simultaneously. When a person experiences this they feel a need to alter one of those cognitions so that they can resolve the dissonance, therefore regaining consistency in their thoughts. This also happens when we engage in new behaviours. We look to ourselves to explain why we do what we do. So if you can get a person to do something for you they need to explain it to avoid experiencing cognitive dissonance.

On a practical level, whenever someone asks you for a favour it suggests that they trust you. They're demonstrating a vulnerability that is evidence of at least some positive thoughts towards you. This, in turn, makes it easier for you to like them, because you perceive that they must like you. Of course, asking someone for lots of favours doesn't work, as that's seen as taking advantage, and it's certainly not very effective in building a better relationship. Therefore it's important to practise this habit wisely.

10. Focus on how they feel

As we live in an information-rich society, it can be quite easy to lose ourselves in the content of our conversations. The reality, however, is that people remember you when you make them feel something. They regard you as charismatic when you move them. Emotions are the order of the day, and the very best speakers, salespeople, politicians and teachers know this. They spend more time focusing on affecting the mood or emotional state of their audience than on trying to convey a logical argument or message.

If you really want to become a masterful communicator you should make a habit of paying attention automatically to how other people feel, and your focus should always be on helping them to feel better as a result of your interaction. Most sales that are made are based on feeling, and most people become regular customers of a brand because of how it makes them feel.

Before every interaction you have with someone ask yourself, 'What can I do to make this person feel good?' There could be a million ways to help them feel good, but if you can think of just a couple you will find yourself coming across in a more powerful way, and they will want to be around you more. It's that simple.

11. Say it clearly

Clarity is something you'll see mentioned a lot in this book. That's because being an engaging and compelling communicator has to begin with being clear about what you're saying. If people don't understand your message they can't understand its importance. If you want to impact people you need to ensure that you speak in such a way that anyone could understand you.

The very best speakers know this, and you can see it applied in lots of different situations. Even if you think about the most convincing or most charismatic people you know, chances are that they're really easy to understand. They explain whatever they're speaking about in a way you remember and find easy to convey to someone else. This is what allows their influence to spread. The clearer your message is delivered, the more people will be impacted by it.

So when you find yourself trying to get through to someone, or if you have a message you want to spread, check first how you can articulate it as clearly as possible. What are you really looking to say? What do you really want to know? What do you really want them to do? Answer these questions, identify the clear message and you'll get through to people more easily, and they'll listen to you more.

12. Acting smooth

Acting smooth involves doing things in your own time and making your behaviours and movements more deliberate and purposeful. When you watch the coolest, most sophisticated and smoothest people in movies, the way they move and the way they do things conveys this impression. Their movements are often slow and uninhibited, making everything look so easy.

If you look at some of the great politicians being interviewed, they always pause and answer every question in a composed way. Calmness has a reassuring quality, and when you speak in an even, deliberate and relaxed way you tend to sound more believable. The more unflappable you are, the more competent you are perceived to be and the more confident an impression you create.

People may wonder unconsciously about why you're so relaxed, and often they will conclude that you're sure of what you're saying. That projected competence makes you even more compelling a person to listen to and makes it more likely that people will want to keep doing so.

THE 'HABITS OF SUCCESS' EXERCISE
When you meet people, practise asking the following questions:

Remember them, not just their name
What kind of things are important to the people you meet?

Show that you care
How can you infuse more passion into how you speak?

Demonstrate competence
What are you good at? How can you show people that?

Get into their shoes
What's it like thinking about the world from the other person's perspective?

Start the ball rolling
How can you make the first move? What's the most appropriate introduction?

Pay attention to everyone
Who is important here? What do I want them to say after I'm gone?

Questions are the answer
What questions could you ask to get to know the other person better?

Give genuine praise
What's a genuine compliment that you could give to someone?

Ask for help
How can another person (who you want to influence) help you?

Focus on how they feel
What do you want them to feel? How can you do that?

Say it clearly
What's your message in one sentence?

Acting smooth
How can you look cooler and more effortless in how you communicate?

Chapter 12

The power of a good impression

The happiest conversation is that of which nothing is distinctly remembered, but a general effect of pleasing impression.

SAMUEL JOHNSON

It was a Saturday evening in 2004 and I was sitting in a trendy bar just off Princes Street in the heart of Edinburgh. My training partner and friend, Brian Colbert, was sitting with me, as we had just finished teaching an NLP practitioner course there and were out for a celebratory drink.

Brian, very happily married, and I, inexplicably single, were discussing the topic of body language and flirting. Having studied charisma for a few years, I explained that I felt I was indeed a pretty good flirt. Brian dared me to show him, and so, not wanting to look bad, I decided to take him up on his challenge.

A few minutes later a woman walked into the bar, and I briefly made eye contact with her. She smiled. Immediately she walked over to the bar. I could see her friends greet her there, and they left her at the bar while they made their way past our table. I knew she would soon follow, so this was my chance. I said to Brian, 'Hey, you see that girl over there at the bar with her back to us?' Brian nodded. 'Well, I'm going to give her a smile and wink when she walks past, and she's going to smile a bright smile back.' Brian nodded in approval. The challenge was on.

I waited as she ordered her drink. I decided to loosen up my face muscles and practised a few exercises. I scrunched up my face and stretched it and stretched out my neck. And I waited and waited. I was going to knock her out with my smile. Then she turned from the bar. I got ready. I leaned my head forward. She walked in the direction of our table. I was ready. I was set. Then she made eye contact . . .

You know when you try too hard to do something and end up miserably failing? Like you're trying to fall asleep and the more you try, the more you feel wide awake? Well, that's what happened. As I tried to smile, my face contorted into an expression that must have looked like an angry Gollum from *The Lord of the Rings*. As she approached she saw my crazy attempt at a smile, looked at me in horror and passed by our table as quickly as she could without spilling her glass of wine. Devastatingly for me, Brian saw the entire exchange and started laughing in convulsions. He found himself in tears and almost fell off his chair. He thought it was one of the funniest things he'd ever seen. I, as you might imagine, did not!

That experience taught me the importance of not trying too hard when creating a first impression. It taught me to focus on making the other person feel good rather than on dazzling them with my smile. As ever, there are many conflicting reports as to how long it takes a person to create a first impression of you. Suggestions range from milliseconds to three minutes. One thing is sure, however: for the most part, we make up our mind about a person pretty quickly. This insight is crucially important in business as well as in social interactions.

Your reputation is made up of the way other people see you and of how they think and feel about you. This will be affected by the impressions they form of you in your interactions. There are two types of impression I will consider: first impressions and lasting impressions. First impressions are how the other person perceives you in the beginning. They're extremely important, as they will affect how someone filters everything about you from then on. Lasting impressions refer to things that stick in a person's mind about you.

Since charisma is an impression you create in the mind of another person, it's vital to understand how to deliberately create your desired impression in another person's mind. The confirmation bias we discussed earlier (see chapter 2) suggests that we look for evidence to confirm what we think is correct and dismiss evidence that contradicts it. Despite the importance of the first impression, you can change it if you work hard enough on it.

Furthermore, another logical fallacy, the 'halo effect' (a term coined by the psychologist Edward Thorndike), causes us to attribute, without actual evidence, additional positive characteristics to a person we already admire. For example, studies have been done on the effect of physical attractiveness on the perception of personality. Time and time again, research points to the idea that people who are perceived as more attractive tend to get more favourable personality qualities attributed to them . . . which is really good news for me!

People form their impressions of you according to how you dress, walk, look and talk; on your voice, accent, sense of confidence and sense of cheerfulness; and on other sensory factors of perception (how they see you, hear you, feel you and smell you). Managing your first impression by paying attention to these qualities and presenting yourself in the best possible way will give you a strong advantage.

So let's look at some of the things you need to do to make the best kind of first impression in the minds of other people. Firstly, there are specific physical things you can do to put yourself across in the best light ('impression gestures'). Secondly, there are general behaviours to master in order to connect in the best way with the other person ('impression habits').

IMPRESSION GESTURES
Smile
It's basic and simple, yet it's not always done. Often, because of our nerves, we can fail to smile and instead give off a stressed expression that makes people feel uneasy. By forcing yourself to smile at people when you meet them for the first time, you not only help yourself feel better but you make them feel more welcomed too. Remember, of course, not to do an 'Owen flirting' smile—unless you want to get rid of somebody very quickly!

Be open
Be aware of your body language and make it as open as you can. Smile lots and use open gestures when you want people to feel that you're approachable. When they introduce themselves, be genuinely enthusiastic and accepting. The best way to do this is to have your hands open and your arms by your side and to ensure that your torso is pointing towards the other person. As just explained, a big smile helps make you look open too. Being closed is when you're turned away from the other person, your arms and legs are crossed and your face has a scowl on it.

Compliment sincerely

People remember compliments. They'll remember when you say really nice things, as long as you really mean them. The key is to be genuine and to compliment selflessly. You're simply looking for them to feel good. The better they feel, the nicer their first impression of you will be.

Touch them

A fascinating experiment conducted by Michael Lynn, Joseph-Mykal Le and David Sherwyn in 1998 found that tips in a Bennigan's restaurant in Texas increased significantly when the waiters touched their customers briefly while interacting with them. The average was found to be 11½ per cent with no touching and 15 per cent with brief touching, though what was said in both cases was exactly the same.

The field of examining how we communicate with others through touch is called 'haptics'. The meaning of a touch is heavily dependent on culture and context. In places I've been in the Middle East, as far east as Afghanistan, I've seen men interlock arms or hold hands—completely acceptable behaviour for two men in these places; in the Western world, such touching is often seen as a sign of romantic attachment.

Some interpretations of Judaism and Islam suggest that you should never touch another person's wife in any way. When we're touched by a person, we experience a form of connection with them. We even use the metaphor to 'touch someone', which is a physical sensation, when we talk about affecting their feelings. If culturally acceptable and if in the right context, when talking with someone brush their arm or touch their foot with yours. Make it seem as if you're focused on what you're talking about and casually touch them with your arm or hand—obviously in a non-intrusive place. It will give them a sense that you feel personally close to them.

Charismatic eyes

In business or personal life, connecting with someone happens primarily through the eyes.

In a corporate setting practise keeping eye contact a second or two longer than normal and smile. It conveys confidence and suggests that you're really present and fully focused on the other person. When you look into a person's eyes it creates a sense of intimacy, and this can help you build better rapport with them.

From a personal standpoint, it's common (in a romantic context) to look at someone and then, when they see you, to look away. Instead, practise holding their gaze for a few seconds and smiling. This indicates that you're confident and very secure in yourself, and it acknowledges them positively. Also, look for something that you find attractive about someone. If you genuinely perceive something attractive, you will smile in an irresistible way. But do remember that there's a difference between gazing and staring: gazing is the seed of a deeper connection; staring is the seed of a restraining order.

Handshake

When shaking hands with another person your grip should be neither too firm nor too weak. I'm always amazed at most men, who try and crush the other person's hand. Unless you actually want them hating you, it's best to avoid it.

Make sure you shake hands at medium strength, as if you were giving them a really good feeling through your hands. A nice smile and eye contact works wonders as you're doing this.

IMPRESSION HABITS
Be confident

People remember confidence, so the more you feel self-confident and charming in their presence, the more you will be remembered for being attractive. From the earlier chapters you will have understood the importance of having a confident attitude and state of mind when communicating with others.

Be funny

People remember humour, so the more you make them laugh, the more they will remember you positively. In chapter 20 you will learn how to be funnier and make people laugh.

Be interesting

People remember good stories, so the more you entrance them with your tales, the more they will want to meet you again. Storytelling is another skill you will learn to improve later in this book (see chapter 21). Since we tell stories all the time, your ability to make yours interesting will have a significant impact on how people feel about you when they meet you for the first time.

Be kind

People remember generosity, kindness and good manners. They also remember stinginess, meanness and bad manners. So the more you behave like a gentleman or a lady, the more positive their impression of you will be. The key is to do so without being a walkover. A perfect blend of kindness and self-confidence works wonders. You will find that you will behave like that naturally when you start learning to like yourself more.

Be graceful under pressure

People remember how you respond under pressure, so the more you demonstrate confidence and grace in tough situations, the more they will form a positive impression of you. Sometimes the first time you meet someone will be in a high-pressure environment. If you can stay calm and collected it will give you an air of authority and leadership and make them more likely to be influenced by you.

Treat them as important

People remember how friendly you were and whether you remembered their names and other facts about them, so the more you call them by their name and ask them questions about their life, demonstrating that you remember what they told you, the more they will perceive you as a considerate, sympathetic person. Demonstrating that you care enough to regard their life as important is really effective at winning people over. Of course, you should genuinely care and not fake it!

Be on time

People remember tardiness and lateness. Always make sure you're on time or early. Being late for someone, especially the first time you meet, can be a sign of disrespect. If they're waiting a long time for you they will start judging you, and they will see your tardiness as a sign that you don't value their time as much as your own.

Be clean and groomed

Society values cleanliness and good hygiene, so always make sure to be groomed immaculately. Pay special attention to the small details. From working in Milan, the fashion capital of the world, I have experience of learning the importance of everything from matching socks to the way you wear your suit. Everything matters, so pay attention to it. Even if they don't notice consciously, people will often notice unconsciously.

Make them feel special

People remember being made to feel special. Always ask yourself, 'How can I make this person feel special?' It works wonders. It could be doing something extra for them, giving a small gift or compliment, or helping them in some way. Even something small helps them feel like the meeting is important to you.

Primacy and recency effect

The first and last things you say are always more likely to be remembered. That's important to bear in mind when you communicate with others. Make sure to say what you most want the person to remember at the beginning and end of a conversation. Even if the whole conversation doesn't go how you want it to, focus on ensuring that what you start with and finish with are memorable and really positive.

How to change a first impression

If you've found yourself getting off to a rocky start with someone, there are a number of things you can do to change the impression they've made in their mind about you. Firstly, you can acknowledge how you might have come across to them when you met them previously. You can then explain it away with a joke or a compliment for them. For example, if you think they saw you as arrogant on your first meeting, you can say something like, 'Hi, I want to start by apologising if I came across a little cocky the first time we met. It's just I took too many happy pills' (joke). Or you could say, 'It's just I was kind of nervous about meeting you—I've heard so many great things about you' (compliment).

Another strategy is to figure out exactly what kind of person they think you are and to act in the completely opposite way on your second meeting, so that they have to re-evaluate you. Whichever approach you use, concentrate on what you like about the other person, as it will help you to come across as more genuine and more likeable.

Chapter 13

How to read others easily: Decoding people

Fie, fie upon her!
There's language in her eye, her cheek, her lip;
Nay, her foot speaks. Her wanton spirits look out
At every joint and motive of her body.

WILLIAM SHAKESPEARE

It was about five o'clock on a Thursday evening in the state of Nevada. I looked around the table. There were nine other players, all of them characters, some of them stereotypes. There was the old lady with the feathered hat and the cigarette dangling from her mouth. There was the young Latino wearing a striped grey suit, hair slicked back. There was the guy in his fifties with receding grey hair, wearing dark sunglasses. We were in a casino in Las Vegas and we were playing poker.

Now, I'm not much of a gambler. In fact, I'm not much of a poker player. Put me online and I will, more than likely, lose. And lose big. I struggle to remember which hands win, and my ability to calculate odds has never been honed. Put me in a game for half an hour and, again, I will, more than likely, lose. But that day the circumstances were different. I had one skill that would allow me to triumph.

Before going to the table, I had tried my hand at a number of slot machines and blackjack tables. I had decided on a limit of five hundred dollars, and I had just lost four hundred. So I bought chips for a game of poker and settled in. After an hour I had lost all my chips, and I was asked if I'd like to buy back in. Now, at that stage I was close to getting up from the table and walking away. But I didn't.

I stayed—not because I got lost in some addictive need to continue but because I just noticed something.

On my final hand, I had called a bluff from the man in the sunglasses. I'd seen him bluff a number of times. But then he produced the goods: I noticed he did something he hadn't done in any of his other bluffs. The previous three times he went for it he smirked slightly. This time, though, his face was unchanged as he made his move.

The psychologist in me had to find out if my instinct was right. You see, the whole hour I had been studying each player and monitoring their body language and gestures. I had been watching them closely and paying attention to every cue. I lost for an hour, but once I bought back in, everything changed. Not only was I right about the man in the sunglasses but I was right about the others as well. They watched in surprise as the Irish guy who'd been getting trounced made back all his money (including the amount I'd lost elsewhere in the casino). Then, after two-and-a-half hours at the table, I walked away.

When people hear that story they ask me (usually with sarcasm!) why I don't just go into being a poker player if I'm so good. My answer is simple: I'm not necessarily good at poker, only one part of it. The very best players are good at all parts of it. The point, though, is that the skills of reading people helped me out, not just that Thursday evening in a Las Vegas casino but in many other situations as well.

In this chapter, I want to explain some rarely revealed facts about how you can get the edge in understanding other people more effectively. Having studied all kinds of human behavioural analysis, from magic to marketing, from CIA methods of interrogation to non-verbal psychology, I want to share with you some of the keys to understanding other people more deeply and more quickly than ever before.

THE IMPORTANCE OF PAYING ATTENTION

One of my favourite television programmes has to be the classic series 'Lie to Me', starring Tim Roth. He plays Cal Lightman, an eccentric psychologist-turned-detective who has mastered the science of body language. Having spent years researching the field of facial expressions, Lightman (incidentally modelled on a real-life researcher, Paul Ekman) helps solve crimes by being able to judge when people are lying. The clever hook was that although he could always tell when someone was lying, he couldn't tell *why* they were, which gave the show lots of traction.

Although probably about only half the body-language 'facts' in it were accurate, the series was very interesting because it prompted the viewer to practise what is by far the most important of all the skills of reading other people: paying close attention to them. Because we were trying to read what Lightman was reading, we would notice every facial expression, every tick or scratch, and wonder what it meant.

But 'Lie to Me' is just one of many fascinating programmes that involve characters studying and reading other people for clues about what's going on. The excellent new British television adaptation of Sherlock Holmes, starring Benedict Cumberbatch, is another great example of this. Rather than focusing on whether or not a person is lying, Holmes looks at every little detail and deduces information from their behaviour, clothes, positioning, words, body language and so on. When Holmes first meets Watson in the series he is introduced to one of Watson's colleagues. Holmes asks for a loan of a mobile phone to check something, so Watson gives it to him. From this, Holmes deduces that Watson is an army doctor who has recently returned from Afghanistan or Iraq and that he has a brother who is worried about him but who won't visit him because he is an alcoholic. He also explains that Watson's limp is psychosomatic. Ridiculous? Well, here's how he does it.

Because of Watson's posture and haircut, Holmes infers that he was in the military. Watson's limp, together with the tan on his hands and face, allows Holmes to deduce that he was injured abroad, in the Middle East. He also deduces that the limp is psychosomatic from the fact that Watson, when he came into the room, didn't automatically look for a chair. Holmes guesses that Watson has a brother because the phone is inscribed *To Harry Watson from Clara*. Since it was given to Harry as a present and then given to Watson, Holmes, noting the recent make and model of the phone, supposes that Watson's brother had only recently split up from Clara. Holmes also concludes that Watson was an army doctor because, on entering the science lab, Watson mentions that it was 'a bit different from my day', suggesting that he had trained in a lab himself. Finally, Holmes guessed that Watson's brother had a problem with alcohol because the phone's charger socket showed signs of having been scratched repeatedly, suggesting that it had been charged by unsteady hands, possibly by someone who is drunk every night (the time of day when the phone needs charging). Watson confirms most of this as fact—except that his brother is actually his sister, Harriet.

Although this is fiction, it's a great example of the fact that there's a lot of information about another person at our disposal, so long as we pay attention to all the details. In many ways the skills of being a detective are similar to the those of reading others. It's about paying attention to all the information and deducing as much as possible.

When I talk about reading or decoding others, I'm not just talking about how people act when they're lying or telling the truth: I'm talking about their appearance, body language, tone of voice, background and so on, and what all that tells you about them. The more you can read and understand others, the better you will be at communicating effectively and connecting with them. Most people find themselves very inwardly focused, and yet, with a small switch of your attention, you can get much more valuable information.

The key to reading people is to ensure that you don't allow one behaviour or aspect of how they come across to dominate your perception. Instead, get into the habit of noticing patterns and make sure that any understanding you allow yourself to develop about someone is based on a number of different aspects in a number of different areas. Reading people is about joining the clusters of clues from the various dimensions together. It's about continually updating what you think about a person according to more and more new evidence. Let's examine the different types of information you can extract from meeting someone.

BODY LANGUAGE (POSTURE, GESTURES, POSITIONING, FACIAL EXPRESSIONS)

Now, like many of the topics I cover in this book, there are many, many things I could write about body language. Indeed, it has a plethora of books dedicated to it alone. But here are some of the most important things to keep in mind when reading a person's posture, gestures, positioning and facial expressions.

It's all about clusters. When you see a number of different signals coming from a person's body language all saying the same thing, it gives you a better understanding of what's really going on for them. Crossed arms by itself means nothing. It's only when you see their arms crossed and a number of other non-verbal and verbal exhibitions of a certain emotion that you can gauge how they're feeling.

We then listen to the words they use in combination with their body, facial and vocal expression, and when the messages are incongruent we get an inkling that something is 'off'. This is also the way to decipher when people are lying. When you become skilled at 'calibration' you can notice someone's communication patterns when they're telling you something that's true and when they're telling you something that's a lie. By noticing these patterns, you develop a useful ability to detect truth and lies, based solely on how people communicate.

So, what are the basics of becoming better at reading body language once you're on the lookout for clusters of information? The first thing to realise is that many physical gestures seem to be hard-wired into the brain. From an evolutionary standpoint, the fight, fright and flight responses tend to have an impact physically as well as physiologically. When we're under stress we react either by standing strong in an effort to establish dominance, by freezing and holding ourselves still or by attempting to flee the situation.

A well-known study was conducted by researchers from Columbia University that examined the gestures of victory and loss of athletes competing in the 2004 Olympic and Paralympic Games. They found a striking correlation in the gestures of those who were victorious and a correlation in the gestures of those who were defeated. The fascinating thing is that many of those studied were in fact blind from birth, so it seems that those particular physical postures and responses are hard-wired into the brain.

The explanation for all this lies in the concept that, instead of having one brain, we actually have three. Firstly, there's the brain stem, or reptilian brain. This is the most basic part of the brain. Secondly, there's the limbic brain. This part includes the hippocampus and the amygdala and is the seat of emotion. Our limbic system enables us to process information extremely quickly so we can protect ourselves if we need to when something is happening. Finally, there's the neocortex, which is the analytical brain. This studies information to draw logical and rational conclusions based on evidence.

When we read someone's body language, the limbic system gives us an instinctive response to it. We then analyse that feeling with our neocortex and can tell whether or not someone is pleased or disappointed, even before we can explain why. We read it automatically. The next thing to understand about body language is that, despite certain gestures being hard-wired, most people are unique and have their own form of non-verbal expression.

What this means is that when trying to read another person's non-verbal cues you should first establish their 'baseline'. This is their default state and refers to how they usually stand, sit or walk. Some people might naturally have certain habits of expressing themselves that are not necessarily related to how they're feeling. When you notice the person you're communicating with, make sure you have a clear baseline to read from.

One of the key elements of body language to be aware of is the position of a person's torso. If they're pointing their body one way and their head another, it's their body position that reveals where their attention is. So if you're speaking to a prospective date and their head is pointing towards you but their body is pointing to some other possibility, the likelihood is that you aren't in with much of a chance! The 'belly-button rule', so-called by Janine Driver in her great book *You Say More Than You Think*, suggests that the direction in which someone's belly button is pointing gives you clues as to what really matters to them.

So, examine the other person's posture. Check their facial expression. Watch where they're pointing their body. Look to see what their gestures seem to be saying and pay attention to whether or not these gestures are aligned with what they're expressing verbally, and to how they're doing so. Doing this will give you a strong advantage in figuring out what their real thoughts are.

APPEARANCE (DRESS, STYLE, GROOMING)
'Appearance' is not simply judging a person by their clothes: it's paying attention to what it tells you about them. When they're interested in someone, most people know to check the fourth finger of the left hand of the person they're chatting to in order to see if they're married or engaged.

The kind of watch a person wears doesn't just tell you if they're rich: if it's an expensive watch, it also tells you that they value showing others a symbol of their success. If they wear a status symbol, they will probably be more likely to judge you by your appearance. The clothes a person wears, their accessories, their shoes, how they wear their clothes, their hair, any body art—all this is information. It doesn't tell you anything conclusively, but it definitely provides clues about the kind of person you're talking to. The secret often lies in the details and, in particular, in the attention to detail.

BACKGROUND (CULTURE, UPBRINGING)

Racial profiling can lead to many problems when used as an excuse to exhibit prejudicial tendencies. Judging a person by the colour of their skin or by their religion is ignorant and immoral. But what's important to remember is the value of learning about a person according to their background. Their nationality, religion or culture can give you valuable information about the kind of person they are. Now, I've met people who are radically different from each other even though they've lived only a few miles apart in Dublin all their lives . . . and I've made friends in North Korea who, though they have never been out of the country, remind me of friends of mine from London. This is not to say that background defines character, but there's useful information to be gleaned from an understanding of a person's background.

What they have been through, what circumstances they have grown up in—everything gives you clues as to why they now do what they do. Again, notice what's actually there and avoid jumping to conclusions. Become a student of the background of others and you'll find yourself extracting a lot of useful information about how best to communicate with them.

VOCAL INFORMATION (VOICE TONE, ACCENT, SPEED)

Because of all the travelling I do, probably one of the skills I've developed best is the art of reading different tones of voice. In most countries I've been to, I can tell from listening to people on the phone whether a person is getting good or bad news, what kind of relationship they have to another person, and, seconds before they do it, when they're about to hang up.

My favourite place to practise this is Japan, since the language is so radically different from English. For example, I noticed that the sound of their vowels tends to become elongated just before they say goodbye (which is similar to what we do in English).

People have a different rhythm when they're speaking to a close friend or family member, to a child or parent, or to a business colleague or client. Their tone varies depending on whether or not they're listening to good news or bad news. A massive amount of communicative information is available in such rhythms.

Listening to how a person says what they say is a really good habit to get into. By noticing a person's tone of voice, you can examine whether or not it's consistent with their body language and the words they're using. Their accent can obviously tell you where they're from and, in some cases, help you understand more about their social status. The speed at which they speak also reveals how they think and how slowly or quickly they process information. Therefore it gives you an indication of the appropriate speed for communicating with them.

LANGUAGE (SENSORY WORDS, INFORMATION, WORD CHOICE)

Paying attention to how a person uses language enables you to understand a lot about how they think. When they speak to you, do they exaggerate or understate when they tell you about something? If they exaggerate it indicates that they're more likely to create dramas out of situations, but this can also be more fun to listen to. If they understate they might sometimes be less engaging, but you can probably talk to them with a lot less drama.

If they talk in a big-picture, high-level kind of way and use more abstract words, it lets you know that they're probably more comfortable with general concepts than with detail. The more specific and concrete their language, the more likely it is that they're more comfortable with detail. This will inform you about how best to explain something to them.

Articulation and diction can also offer you some understanding as to the background of the speaker. It can suggest what kind of school they attended and can reveal their social class. The key is to get used to paying attention to how the person speaks and not only to what they say.

STUFF (POSSESSIONS, ORGANISATION, OFFICE OR LIVING SPACE)

In his book *Snoop: What Your Stuff Says about You*, Sam Gosling, a behavioural scientist, examines how our 'stuff' reveals lots of clues about the kind of people we are. He has conducted many studies on what a person's possessions and the organisation of their home or office can tell us about them. He explains that there are three primary types of information we can gain from examining someone's personal spaces: 'identity claims', 'feeling regulators' and 'behavioural residue'.

Identity claims involve possessions that remind us of who we are or that tell others who we are. For example, in my living-room I have a signed and framed photo of my beloved Glasgow Celtic, the football team I support. This tells anyone who comes into my home that Celtic are important to me and that I'm a supporter. Where you position something also matters. If you have a desk at work and you position an item so that only you can see it, it's likely that you have it to remind yourself of the identity you possess. If it's placed for someone else to see, it suggests that you want them to know how you identify yourself.

Feeling regulators are items you use to change your emotional state. It might be an inspirational poster or a photo of your children. You use it to get yourself into the kind of state you want to be in. This indicates to another person what states are important for you to be in and what feelings you value.

Behavioural residue refers to the traces you leave of what you're doing. For example, how organised your room or car is can give an indication of how much value you place on cleanliness, of how important your room or car is to you, and even of how busy you are. Most of the time, when you do something in your office, information is left behind that tells us more about you. Over time this behaviour can give us a better understanding of your personality.

THE 'HUMAN-READING CHEAT SHEET' EXERCISE
Below are questions to ask yourself whenever you meet someone and want to read them.

> *What is their body language like?*
> *What emotional state does their posture and facial expression suggest?*
> *Where is their body pointing to?*
> *How consistent is their body language with their tone of voice and what they're saying?*
> *What do their gestures convey?*
> *What clusters of body language and gesture all seem to suggest the same things?*
> *How are they dressed? What kind of clothes are they wearing?*

How well groomed are they?

What clues can you get from their background, culture or nationality?

What does their voice tell you about them?

What do the words they use tell you about them?

What do their possessions or personal spaces tell you about them?

Chapter 14
How to win friends: Building rapport

There are two types of people—those who come into a room and say, 'Well, here I am!' and those who come in and say, 'Ah, there you are.'

FREDERICK L. COLLINS

In 1933, Dale Carnegie published one of the classic self-help books, *How to Win Friends and Influence People*, which has become the bible of communication skills. Carnegie offers simple yet effective wisdom on how to get on better with people. His advice includes 'Smile,' 'Don't criticise, condemn or complain,' 'A person's name is the most important word in their language' and 'Give sincere and honest praise.'

Here's the thing: we know all that. It's obvious. Why do people bother buying such a book? The answer: we don't really know all that. We understand that it's the right thing to do, the smart thing to do. But that doesn't mean we do it. Still, eighty years after the book was made available there are plenty of people (millions probably) who lack social skills. We meet them everywhere and complain. 'Bad customer service,' we say, when the reality is that they've simply fallen into the trap of getting so lost in life that they forget they're a part of it.

In more recent times, a writer named Daniel Goleman has popularised the terms 'emotional intelligence' and 'social intelligence'. We all understand that our ability to get on better with people is vital to our success and future happiness. Many people, however, dismiss the 'art form' of making friends as being something we know how to do naturally.

The danger here is that when we dismiss the necessary application of social skills we find ourselves severely limited in how well we can do. You see, winning friends and building rapport is about many of the behaviours that Carnegie outlines. But it's also about learning to connect with others by thinking about the world more and more from their point of view. It's finding the commonality we share with others that enables us to really make a powerful connection with them.

If you've ever been with a person you really got on great with, you've probably noticed that their posture and facial expressions have often matched yours. Have you ever yawned because you saw someone else yawn, or laughed because everyone else was laughing? These are all examples of being in rapport.

Now, there are whole books written about rapport. I've only devoted a small chapter to the subject, because I want to focus on the most important things you need to remember.

Rapport is just like a dance of communication. The key to effective rapport-building is 'subtlety'. Rapport is the process by which we create and develop a positive relationship with another person. It's not always essential, but it's usually very useful to possess it. Rapport works because people like people who are like themselves. When you match and pace a person unconsciously, it enables you to create a subtle connection through which you can lead them into different states. This is the notion of pacing and leading.

PACING AND LEADING

Pacing is the accurate and ongoing matching or mirroring of your external behaviour or language with another person's. By matching your breathing or body posture, or by using the same key words, you develop a strong bond or relationship with that person.

Leading is when, once you've paced a person successfully, you begin to alter your behaviour so that they begin to follow you. At a very basic level, for example, if someone has their arms folded and you fold your arms to match, and then after a few seconds you unfold your arms and they follow you, you've paced and led that behaviour.

EXAMPLES OF RAPPORT

Breathing: Adjust your breathing patterns to match that of the other person.

Body matching: You can mirror another's posture directly, indirectly or partly, or match one part of your behaviour to a different part of theirs (breathing to tonality).

Vocal qualities: Match shifts in tonality, volume, intonation patterns etc.
Facial expressions: You can pay attention to the facial expression a person uses and return them subtly.
Gestures: Matching a person's body gestures in a way that's respectful and elegant.
Verbal: Repeat the phrases the other person likes to use.

The art of rapport really begins with the right intention. Your intention has to be good, and you have to want the other person to get what they want, as well as you getting what you want. I've always found that, unless I had the right intention, no matter how well I paced the other person there would be some obstacle to succeeding in creating rapport with them.

Getting into rapport will enable you to persuade the other person more easily, as they will trust you more and feel they get on better with you. The key is to get your desires to be win-win. When you look for what they want and can connect it with what you want, you put yourself in a really useful place to get on great with them naturally.

Quite often, when faced with a difficult person in a hostile state it's important to develop rapport by getting into a similar state and then focusing on something meaningless. Then you can begin to relax yourself and lead them into a more relaxed state.

For example, I remember being at a party with friends when a fight was about to break out between two men who were both reasonably drunk. I walked between them as they stared each other out, and I started to get furious, directing my rage at the carpet. As I screamed and began angrily thumping it, I gradually calmed down, and eventually I became completely motionless on the ground. Both men looked at me, shook their heads and walked away. Their anger had gone.

Now, I'm not saying you should ever consider doing anything like this. It was pretty extreme and could have got me in more trouble. It's just a good example of rapport working.

REPRESENTATIONAL SYSTEMS
One of the discoveries about human communication that NLP is famous for is the understanding that people generally express themselves in one of three primary modalities. Some people tend to

use more visual words and expressions. They say things like 'The way it looks to me . . .' or 'The way I see it . . .' or 'I'd like you to get a clear picture of what I'm showing you and how it looks from my viewpoint.' Others use more auditory or 'sound' language and say things like 'I hear what you're saying' or 'That resonates with me' or 'Let's talk about it more and discuss it.' Still others use more feeling words (kinaesthetic) and say things like 'I'm getting to grips with what you're giving me here' or 'This doesn't sit well with me' or 'My gut says I can handle this—I feel I will.'

Depending on which type of language the person uses and in which order, you can communicate with them by using in return the same systems in the same sequence. This will ensure that you make them feel as if you're on the same page, because you are, quite literally, speaking the same language.

BREAKING RAPPORT

Getting in rapport is an important skill to learn, but it's also necessary to learn how to break rapport effectively. Breaking rapport is about ending a particular connection with someone when it's no longer useful. For example, have you ever found yourself talking away to someone who was boring you or wasting your time, but you couldn't seem to get away from them?

The art of breaking rapport is simply about mismatching them as well as you can. When you do this, they will unconsciously feel like something isn't right but will not be able to put their finger on it. You can then hijack the conversation and begin to talk, trailing off and explaining that you have to go. That way you can end the conversation without appearing to be rude.

THE 'RAPPORT' EXERCISE

Find someone to talk to and practise the following experiments.

In experiment 1, have a conversation with someone and deliberately mismatch their body language and words. Breathe at a different rate, sit or stand in a different posture, use a different rate of speech, different gestures and different facial expressions. Furthermore, if you've noticed that they're using one representational system more than others, use one of the ones they're not using when replying to them.

Once you've done this, note how the interaction has gone.

In experiment 2, deliberately match their body language and words. Breathe at the same rate at them, sit or stand in the same posture, use the same rate of speech, the same gestures and similar facial expressions. If you've noticed that they're using one representational system more than others, use that one more when replying to them.

Once you've done this, note how the interaction has gone.

What you'll probably find is that in experiment 2 you will have created a far better bond than in experiment 1. The key, then, is to practise using experiment 2 with everyone you meet with whom you want to create rapport.

Chapter 15

Look like this: Style management

Clothes make the man. Naked people have little or no influence on society.

MARK TWAIN

Let's face it. In the beautiful country of Ireland, we're famous for many things: our skills in charming, storytelling, literature, poetry, music and dance; our sense of fun and friendliness; our beautiful scenery and countryside—our good-looking psychologists! But one thing we're not famous for is style. Compared with many other countries, we just don't 'get' style.

Take Italy for example. Having worked there regularly over the last eight years or so, I've learnt many lessons in how to dress. It's not just a case of having to dress up to make a good impression: if you don't dress up and make an effort you'll actively be making a poor impression.

Now, I know many people who resent the fact that your dress sense or style affects the perception that other people will have of you. It's not nice, but that's the way it is, so, unfortunately, you need to pay attention to it. Most people understand that they need to make an effort to dress nicely if they have an interview or are going on a first date. The key is to make dressing well your default state rather than something you motivate yourself to do for 'special occasions'.

It doesn't mean that you need to be an expert. God knows, I'm far from an expert, but there are a number of things I've learnt from spending time with some of the best fashion experts.

If you can, hire a style consultant. If not ask a friend with great dress sense to go shopping with you. Generally I have some female friends and some male friends (mostly either gay or Italian) who help me choose the right kind of clothes. The trick is to pay special attention to those of your friends who tend to dress well and ask them for help. If this isn't an option all the time, there are some basic bits and pieces I've picked up over the years.

Start noticing patterns and get into the habit of noticing when someone else is dressed well. When you see the difference between someone dressing well and dressing poorly you'll start to get better at dressing yourself. It's not just what you wear, it's how you wear it. Accessories matter. Socks matter. Shoes matter. All parts of your wardrobe matter. When you wear a suit make sure it's pressed and looks sharp. Ensure that your shirts look clean and fresh. Learn about colour, what colours suit you and what colours go together. You don't have to be perfect, but recognise that the further away from perfect you are, the more it will affect the other person's perception of you. Also, pay attention to your nails, skin, teeth, feet, hands and hair. Consider everything. Ensure that you present yourself really well at all times.

One great technique is to practise thinking about famous people you look like, or have a similar shape to, who look really well. Start noticing how they dress in photos in magazines and when being interviewed, or even when playing a character in your favourite television programme. Part of making a change in this area involves you starting to pay attention to how other people dress. You can do this when you're out shopping as well. Think about how the people walking past you are dressed and ask yourself how you might look if you were dressed like them.

Learn about the basic fashion rules: dark colours tend to be slimming and also to look warmer, so they're especially good for the winter; bright colours tend to look better in the summer; vertical stripes tend to be slimming; horizontal stripes tend to make you look bigger; heels tend to make you look straighter, taller (obviously) and slightly slimmer; socks should match and never be worn with sandals. It's better to get a small amount of really good clothes than a large amount of poor-quality clothes.

DRESSING FOR THE MIRROR

What's also fascinating about the clothes you choose to wear is the new science of 'enclothed cognition'. Two psychologists, Hajo Adam and Adam Galinski, conducted a study in which they found a difference in behaviour that resulted from the wearing of different types of clothes. When someone wore a lab coat when doing certain problem-solving tasks it improved their performance. In the 1980s and 90s Mark Frank and Tom Gilovich of Cornell University found that National Hockey League teams that wore black committed more fouls and racked up more penalties than those in other colours. It seems that the type of clothes you wear and the colours you choose have an effect on your thoughts, feelings and behaviour (they also have a potential effect on others).

Of course, in many ways we don't need a study to know this. All you have to do is walk past a group of goths and you'll see the subculture of black trench coats and droopy faces linked with the dark tone of that music. Or you could simply notice how you feel about yourself when you're all dressed up for a friend's wedding or when you walk across that dance floor looking like James Bond or Kate Middleton. How you dress doesn't just tell the world about you: it tells you about you. So, dress nicely.

Always look at yourself in the mirror before you go out and ask yourself, 'If I was to see someone dressed like me, what would I think of them?'

It's a good idea to pay close attention to yourself and answer the following questions:

How do you come across?
How do you dress?
What is your grooming and appearance like?
Do you come across as being stylish?

STYLE PLAN

It's important to be aware of the different elements of style. Find someone who knows about it and has a good sense of style themselves and work through the following areas on how you could improve your style. Just write down what improvements you can make. Become more aware of the details.

Hair

_____

_____

_____

_____

_____

_____

Accessories

_____

_____

_____

_____

_____

Clothes

_____

_____

_____

_____

_____

Shoes

_____

_____

_____

_____

_____

Make-up

_____

_____

_____

_____

_____

_____

Aroma

_____

_____

_____

_____

_____

_____

Occasion wear
Very formal (weddings)

_____

_____

_____

_____

_____

_____

Semi-formal (parties)

_____

_____

_____

_____

_____

_____

Going out (night out in town)

_____

_____

_____

_____

_____

_____

Semi-going out (cinema, local pub)

_____

_____

_____

_____

_____

_____

Casual (might pop round to a friend's or to a shop)

_____

_____

_____

_____

_____

_____

Really casual (no intention of going out)

_____

_____

_____

_____

_____

_____

Gym gear (gym clothes, jogging)

_____

_____

_____

_____

_____

_____

Chapter 16

Sound like this: Cultivating a charismatic voice

I talk in that baby talk voice when I'm on TV. It's a put-on.

PARIS HILTON

When I was first hired by RTÉ to work as the presenter of 'Not Enough Hours', I went through hours and hours of training to become more comfortable on camera. I learnt a number of skills for presenting pieces to camera and delivering memorised scripts in a more natural way.

One of the individuals RTÉ hired to work with me was the voice coach Poll Moussoulides. Poll had worked with such Hollywood legends and celebrities as Whoopi Goldberg, Richard Dreyfuss, Pierce Brosnan and Angela Lansbury. He was obviously world class at what he did, and it was a great opportunity to learn from him.

Instantly we hit it off. I learnt a massive amount from Poll about how to use my voice more effectively. One of the things he emphasised was the importance of variety in how I spoke. Being engaging, he explained, means using a diverse range of sounds that ensure you keep the attention of whoever is listening. It's also essential to make sure that there's plenty of variety in your tone so that you can speak with different vocal characteristics to create focus and more fully animate your communication.

It's obvious enough that to sound charismatic you have to learn how to speak in a charismatic way. What this means is that your voice must be able to convey emotion easily through tone and rhythm. So, because breath is the source of all vocal activity, it's important to practise speaking by breathing with all the related muscles activated so that you have the power and support you need.

When you do this, your voice will flow more comfortably and it will also help you to confidently project your voice without feeling like you have to shout. An additional benefit is that the resonance created from a well-produced voice allows sound to easily flow through your body and to be more connected to your message. This improves the quality of your voice, the ease of your delivery and will have a big influence on whether or not people will like to listen to you.

Also, practise doing lots of different things with your voice. Acquire as much vocal flexibility as possible. It will make a great difference to your charismatic appeal. The tone of your voice is a fantastic tool that you can also use to create different states in those with whom you speak. The ability to alter your tone and the rhythm of your voice enables you to create different states (including altered states) in other people.

When you speak to someone, you're bathing them in tonality. It affects their entire body. Therefore by learning to control your tone and tempo you can master your ability to lead people into the states you want them to be in. If you want a person to feel excited you must use an excited tone of voice. If you want them to feel relaxed you must use a relaxed tone. A fast rhythm in your voice won't help someone become more relaxed, but it may help them become more excited and motivated.

The pace at which you speak should never be too far from the pace of those with whom you're communicating. If you're in conversation with someone who is speaking slowly, speak more slowly and enter their world. This will make it easier to create rapport with them.

You can also learn to vary your tone of voice to emphasise some points and discount others. You can use a hesitant tone of voice to describe something, so that you link the feeling of hesitancy to it through verbal anchoring. Every tone of voice you have conveys a particular feeling. You can use the various tones to create different kinds of anchor and associate them with the ideas you speak of to others.

You can use a deliberate pause after making an important point to make it sound particularly significant. You can give a falling inflection to your sentences to make them affect the brain like a command; it makes you sound more certain. When you use a rising inflection it makes the sentence affect the brain like a question. When you use a neutral tone it affects the brain like a statement.

You can practise using different accents. The more accents you can do, the more entertaining and powerful your stories will become. Instead of merely describing what a person said, you will be able to impersonate them so that the story will have more dramatic appeal and become infinitely more amusing.

Pay attention to the following:
- the *resonance* (quality) of your voice
- your *tone* (feeling) of voice
- the *rhythm* and *tempo* of your voice
- the *inflection* of your voice
- the *variety* of your voice.

THE 'SOUNDING CHARISMATIC' EXERCISE

Practise recording your voice and get used to speaking from your diaphragm to ensure that most of your body resonates and vibrates when you speak. Also practise speaking in the following tones of voice and convey the emotion with each tone:
- happy
- sad
- tired
- excited
- energised
- passionate
- interested
- curious
- playful
- focused.

Practise speaking in different kinds of rhythm. Listen to the way people speak and sort the voices for the different kinds of rhythm. It's not that important how you describe the differences. What's important is that you notice them and can use the different kinds of rhythm on purpose.

Practise using inflection to mark out different words, practise using falling inflection to induce certainty and practise rising inflection to induce doubt.

Listen to ten different accents and practise mastering each one. Listen to the accent and repeat it to yourself out loud. Do this and alter your voice until you notice that you've developed the accent successfully. A good tip is to be aware of how the person uses their mouth and posture and to listen for the rhythm they use, as that will help you mimic the voice successfully. Never do this in front of the person you're mimicking!

Chapter 17

Walk this way: Charismatic body language

Words are a wonderful form of communication,
but they will never replace kisses and punches.

ASHLEIGH BRILLIANT

On a cool evening on 26 September 1960, more than seventy million American viewers tuned in to watch Senator John F. Kennedy and Vice-President Richard Nixon in the first televised presidential debate ever.

Reports suggest that Nixon arrived in a shirt that didn't fit him, exhausted and tired after having been sick for the past few weeks. Kennedy, on the other hand, had been campaigning in California and enjoyed a tanned and healthy complexion.

In content, the candidates seemed to be evenly matched. But the opinion polls conducted afterwards pointed to Kennedy as victor. What was interesting was the announcement by researchers that Kennedy had been regarded as having won by the television viewers, while Nixon was declared the winner by radio listeners. This soon became widely cited in the media and in the areas of political science and psychology.

More than twenty-five years later two academics, David L. Vancil and Sue D. Pendell, suggested that this 'finding' was not based on valid data. They pointed out the small size of the sample and argued that there wasn't enough evidence to conclude that there was a discrepancy between what the viewers and the radio listeners felt about the debate.

However, what's obvious to anyone who sits down and watches the debates (they're available on YouTube) is that Kennedy came across far better than Nixon. While Kennedy looks composed and relaxed, Nixon looks agitated and sweaty. Indeed, the candidates themselves regarded the debate as having had a powerful impact on people's minds.

Perhaps one of the most quoted studies on body language was conducted by Albert Mehrabian in 1967. The finding suggests that body language accounts for 55 per cent of the effect of a message, voice tone for 38 per cent and the words themselves only 7 per cent. Again, this study has been criticised for being too limited in how it was conducted and for the size of its sample. But this is not to say that the findings should be ignored.

Other studies conducted by Michael Argyle in 1970 and 1988 found body language to be particularly important in the effect it had on the message. In the 1990s David McNeill found that body language during communication could actually underline, undermine or even contradict what someone says. This work was followed by that of Spencer Kelly. In a number of studies conducted since 2007 he showed that when people listen to words that are mismatched to gestures they experience confusion and what he describes as a 'hiccup' in brain function.

Like most psychological findings, there's evidence to both support and detract from the idea that body language is powerful. The reality is that we don't need a study to tell us how important body language is. If you've ever seen someone say they're happy even though their head is tilted downwards and they look miserable, you will realise that you don't believe them. And if you really want to test this, try telling your partner that you love them while shaking your head and looking at them with disgust. Are you willing to give this a go? Thought not!

We've already looked at how your body language actually affects how you feel at a neurological level. So you're aware that the way you walk, stand, sit, move and speak sends signals to your mind about how you're feeling. This means that by changing your body language and your non-verbal behaviour you will have an impact on the way you feel.

Yet what's probably more obvious is the importance of changing your body language in order to present a better impression to other people. As we've learnt from the chapter on reading people (chapter 13), you can gain a lot of information from looking at the body language of other people. Therefore people learn a lot from watching your body language too, which means that it's critical that you know exactly how you can use it to position yourself in the most charismatic way.

Of course, there's no single way of walking, standing or sitting that 'looks charismatic', but there are certain gestures and postures that convey a feeling of confidence and certainty. There are smiles that convey cheerfulness and playfulness, and the speed and rhythm of your walk can convey how relaxed or motivated you are. So the way you move your body will control how charismatically you present yourself to others.

Now, there are ways in which you can begin to look more charismatic. I'm sure you've noticed that there are certain people who walk into a room and make everyone's head turn. Quite often, being good-looking causes this to happen. (Happens to me a lot. Okay, it doesn't. But it should!)

There are many cases, though, where people who would not ordinarily be considered physically attractive stand out. Similarly, there are people who would usually be regarded as attractive who would not be noticed much at all. So attractiveness may help, but it's by no means the most important factor when it comes to making heads turn.

Looking more charismatic means that you convey through your body language the charismatic states we talked about earlier. Once you enter into these states, by using your imagination to create the necessary feelings, you will naturally change your posture to reflect it. As you change your physiology it will have more impact.

This is because of the fact that when you get your body to stand, sit or move confidently it gives signals to your brain to be confident that you can actually make this all work in a cycle. So the key is to make every step you take, every move you make, every word you speak, convey confidence. Confidence is just one of the charismatic states we're talking about.

We've all heard or used the expression 'That person has style.' However, the style I'm talking about is not just style in the sense of the clothes you wear (as we've already discussed): it's the *je ne sais quoi* of a person that makes them particularly appealing.

Most of the communication we engage in is through our body language and tone of voice. We can get a sense of what mood people are in and of what they really mean by noticing their gestures and the tone they use to say something. Standing tall, straight and smiling are signs often conveyed by charismatic people.

Also important is congruence, that is, the process whereby the same meaning of a message is carried by every part of you. The words you use are stated as richly as possible (for example, when you say 'relax' you say it in a calm, relaxed voice). Expressing language with clarity and feeling can contribute powerfully to affecting others. It enables you to inspire and move them more significantly, as well as to construct yourself as a genuine, sincere person.

Every part of your body speaks. The more you line up your body language with what you have to say, the more impact the communication will have on other people. When you speak with congruence you will present people with more unconscious truth, and they will be more affected by your words.

Another important aspect of body language is that the more you use it to express how you feel, the more likely it is that others will feel what you're feeling. The experience, known as the 'emotional contagion phenomenon', occurs when one person feels a certain way and influences others around them. This was described decades ago in the development of NLP, and scientists have since suggested reasons why this occurs. The discovery of brain cells called 'mirror neurons' suggests that when you see someone experiencing an emotion, or when you see them do something, your brain gives you a sense of what this experience would be like. That's why watching people on a big screen kissing, or seeing someone being tortured, has a powerful, visceral effect on us.

What this teaches us is that, whatever our body language is, it should be in alignment with what we want an audience to feel. When you want them to feel confident in what you're saying you must feel confident as well. When you want them to be passionate or motivated, your body language must suggest passion and motivation. The key is that this kind of body language must be congruent. People will know when you're faking it.

Looking charismatic comes down to how you walk and use your gestures and posture, the angles at which you sit or stand, the movement of your head, the way you smile, the way you use your eyes and the way you use your tone of face. Pay attention to the following:

- the way you *walk*
- the way you use your *hand gestures*
- the way you use your *posture* (sitting and standing)
- the *angles* you present

- the movement of your *head*
- the way you *smile*
- the way you use your *eyes*
- the way you use your *tone of face* (facial expression).

THE 'LOOKING CHARISMATIC' EXERCISE
How do you walk when you're at your most charismatic?

_____

_____

_____

_____

_____

_____

How do you gesture with your hands when you're at your most charismatic?

_____

_____

_____

_____

_____

_____

What is your posture when you're at your most charismatic?

_____

_____

_____

_____

_____

_____

What angles do you move at when you're at your most charismatic?

_____

_____

_____

_____

_____

_____

How do you move your head when you're at your most charismatic?

_____

_____

_____

_____

_____

_____

How do you smile when you're at your most charismatic?

_____

_____

_____

_____

_____

How do you use your eyes when you're at your most charismatic?

_____

_____

_____

_____

_____

What is your tone of face like when you're at your most charismatic?

_____

_____

_____

_____

_____

Chapter 18

Talk this way: The language of charisma

I had a linguistics professor who said that it's Man's ability to use language that makes him the dominant species on the planet. That may be. But I think there's one other thing that separates us from animals. We aren't afraid of vacuum cleaners.

JEFF STILSON

One of my mentors in the use of language is Joel Roberts, a media coach who has worked with many celebrities, preparing them for big television interviews in the United States. Joel teaches fantastic courses on what he calls the 'language of impact'. In them he explains that to truly stand out and impact people, you need to learn how to present your idea in a quick and very memorable way. This involves learning media skills that enable you to create sound bites and vivid ways of conveying your message so that it sticks in the mind of every viewer and listener.

These skills of being able to articulate yourself in a masterful way, concisely and vividly, are useful not only in the media but in every context you find yourself in. In his excellent book *Microstyle*, Christopher Johnson explains how we are now more than ever getting used to communicating in short bites of information. Twitter is one such example: you have to communicate your message in just 140 characters. The language of charisma is about learning to do this but also about understanding, once you've got someone's attention in a short space of time, how you can impact them further the more you speak to them. It's about knowing how to use language in everyday conversations to affect the way people feel and what they're thinking about.

In this chapter, I want to explore the power of words, show you how you can grab and keep the other person's attention, and explain what makes them remember what you say.

The words you use have immense power. When you choose the right word at the right time, it can turn a conversation around. When you use the wrong word at the wrong time, it can have an extremely negative impact on your life. Becoming more charismatic also involves you taking deliberate control over how you use language.

There are certain words that move people, inspire people, affect people. There's a way of using language that the most successful speakers on the planet know about. There are words that make a real impact—charismatic words. So how can you begin to use language more charismatically?

SIMPLICITY

We live in a world where the use of sophisticated language seems to be cherished. In business, acronyms and specialised jargon are the order of the day, and often I hear conversations that seem to make absolutely no sense whatsoever. The most charismatic communicators I've met all have the following characteristic in common: they understand the importance of simplicity and of making what they say understandable to absolutely anybody.

CLARITY

Along with simplicity, clarity is an essential ingredient of a memorable message from a charismatic communicator. When you're confused about what someone is saying it's harder to understand where they're coming from or what they want. There's a lack of direction, a lack of leadership. Clarity not only aids understanding but aids recall as well. If you want to be as effective as possible it's important to take responsibility for the message you're communicating and for the clarity of that message. It's up to you to get the message across in the clearest way possible.

METAPHORS

Metaphors are figures of speech that allow you to compare two objects or ideas by presenting them as being the same on some level of comparison. The use of metaphors is critical to being an engaging speaker and is a powerful way of arousing emotions and making your ideas more vivid. They have been shown by studies, such as that by Jay Conger in 1991, to be used effectively to inspire people. In 2005, Jeffrey Mio and his colleagues studied the use of metaphors by past American presidents—from George Washington to Bill Clinton—and found a correlation between the number of metaphors used in their inaugural address and the level of charisma ascribed to them. They also found that the more metaphors that were used in each speech, the more inspirational it was felt to be.

Examples of famous speeches that use powerful metaphors are Winston Churchill's 'iron curtain' speech and Martin Luther King's 'I have a dream' speech. Another well-known metaphor is Shakespeare's 'All the world's a stage, I And all the men and women merely players.'

Metaphors are used every day. But as well as bringing powerful images to mind in wondrous ways, they have also been used in 'loaded language' to ascribe negative traits to certain people in order to promote genocide. Hitler used the terms 'vermin', 'rats' and 'devils' to refer to Jewish people. The Hutu people used the term 'cockroach' to describe the Tutsis during the genocide in Rwanda in 1994.

Metaphors allow us to stand out and really impact others by borrowing from the vividness that comes with more dramatic images. So, in summary, here are the three essential guidelines to being more engaging with your language: (1) be simple, (2) be clear and (3) use metaphors.

Once you've practised the habits of creating the best kind of impression when you meet people—reading people more effectively; building rapport more easily; finding your own style; and using your words, body language and tone of voice to make a bigger impact on the people you speak to—you will find yourself starting to really step forward and present to the world your very best self. The most charismatic communicators have all mastered one particular ability to impact others. You can be charismatic from the inside out and create the best kind of impressions, but the next stage is about the skills you can learn to help you stand out and develop even more of a charismatic edge.

Part 3

Stand out: The art of charisma

Whatever we learn to do, we learn by actually doing it.

ARISTOTLE

On a warm summer evening in Washington, a man stepped up in front of a crowd of more than 250,000 people. They had been waiting for hours to hear him speak, spending much of their time listening to the chorus of speakers that preceded him and to a line-up of such musical stars as Bob Dylan and Pete Seeger. The exact location was in front of the Lincoln Memorial in the heart of the city. The date was 28 August 1963. The man was Martin Luther King, Jr.

To this day King is revered by many and regarded as one of the greatest speakers of all time. In my book, he is simply the best. All I have to do is hear that melodic 'I have a dream' speech and the hairs stand up on the back of my neck, and tears come to my eyes. If ever there was an example of someone blessed with a natural gift for portraying himself in a charismatic way, it is him.

That said, it was on this summer's evening that we also got a glimpse into how charisma works. We got to see, in that very speech, something happen that illuminated how magic was created, for the speech King gave that night differed in the final five minutes from the one he had intended to give. About eleven minutes into his speech, he paused as the crowd clapped. During the applause, Mahalia Jackson, a gospel singer King knew well, shouted from the crowd, 'Tell them about the dream, Martin. Tell them about the dream.' Jackson was referring to part of a speech King had delivered on the road only two months previously. In that moment in Washington, his instinct said she was right. He pushed aside the notes for his prepared speech and began the famous 'I have a dream' passage. This was a wonderful example of what constitutes real charisma. The ability to recite by heart multiple passages and make them blend seamlessly together on the spot was a skill King had mastered, according to Clarence B. Jones, an organiser and colleague of King's.

The magic existed in King's ability to judge the moment and present to the crowd something he felt would resonate with them powerfully. He delivered the passage with the same rhetorical skill that made him so incredible to listen to. Indeed, it was this raw genius that enabled him to perform so marvellously.

Here's what you might not have realised: this genius can be learnt. You see, intuition itself is a skill you practise and master. By that time, King's intuition had been finely tuned.

Having transformed your attitude about yourself and how you can interact with the world, you can, by being more charismatic, attain a sense of freedom that might have escaped you for quite some time. This sense of freedom exists in the knowledge that you are far more than you might have thought, and that you can impact other people far more than you thought you could.

Learning the actions of charisma can certainly help you to do this even more effectively. Your ability to walk, talk, speak and dress in the most engaging way, as well as your ability to read other people and create rapport with them, can make a huge difference to your life.

Inspiring charisma, however, is a rare skill that sets the very best speakers and communicators apart from all the rest. It's the mastery of one of a number of types of ability that enables a person to really affect the world with their charisma.

In truth, there are different kinds of charismatic individuals who are charismatic for different reasons. Some are charismatic because they're very funny, some because they're really interesting, some because they're charming or persuasive and some because they're captivating speakers. I want to explain what I've learnt from studying the most persuasive sales and marketing executives, top comedians, Hollywood screenwriters and prize-winning novelists, as well as some of the best speakers the world has even seen—from world leaders and civil-rights activists to motivational speakers.

I want to uncover the psychology of influence, the factors that make people funny, the keys to compelling storytelling and the fundamentals of delivering a dynamic speech.

Chapter 19
How to influence people

There is nothing in the world like a persuasive speech to fuddle the mental apparatus and upset the convictions and debauch the emotions of an audience not practised in the tricks and delusions of oratory.

MARK TWAIN

In the work I've done over the years, the occasions on which I've spoken to people who are suicidal are among the most dramatic and important work I find myself involved in. It's the ultimate 'sales pitch', getting a person to see why they should continue to live. It's not easy, and it requires you to master the ability to influence. When I find myself in such a situation, there are certain things I know I need to do. The art of influence is what makes the difference.

In this chapter, I want to share with you the 'needle-movers' of influence. What are the most important things you need to know in order to influence other people? From world-class speakers to the very best leaders, the ability to influence and persuade other people is a skill set regarded as fundamentally necessary in life and business. Here we will explore the most important elements of becoming a more influential person.

One of the characteristics associated with charismatic individuals is their amazing ability to convince anyone of anything. When people try to explain why they bought a product, or why they invested their money, they will often use the excuse that the sales consultant or adviser had a lot of 'charisma'. Indeed, more often than not, a presidential candidate with the greatest amount of charisma tends to win the presidency.

So when we look at influence from a charismatic viewpoint, what are the most essential elements to understand in mastering that skill? Well, in this chapter, you will learn about the psychology of influence and persuasion. You will discover what really gets people to change their mind and how your charismatic presence can connect with your audience and win their hearts and minds. You will also find information about the use of charismatic language and some tools from NLP that are very effective in assisting you to change a person's attitude and point of view on something. Finally, you will discover the power of understanding your audience and how they think so that you can be more strategic in how you talk to people.

THE PSYCHOLOGY OF INFLUENCE

The psychology of influence is made up of four elements.

The **source** of a message is who is delivering the message. In this case it will be you, so you have to present and position yourself in the best possible way for the other person. Source also refers to how you manage your own emotional state.

The **message** itself involves two main issues: what you want them to know and how you want them to feel. The message and feeling are equally important, because the emotion will affect whether or not they 'get' the message and so will determine whether or not they will act accordingly.

The **medium** is how the message is presented, that is, in what channel. There are different things to remember about communicating, whether in written form, by phone, face to face or in a presentation.

The **audience** is who you're speaking to. It's important to be aware of how they're thinking and feeling, as well as of what their needs and expectations are, so that you can best get through to them.

I want now to explain how to influence people more effectively by means of each of these four elements.

THE SOURCE (YOU)

Before a word leaves your mouth, the person you're talking to has already been evaluating you and everything they seem to know about you. They might not have been doing it accurately, but they have been unconsciously trying to gauge if you're worth listening to. So it's absolutely critical that you understand how to position yourself in the best possible way to influence and persuade whoever you want to. So, to start with, let's explore the mindset and attitude of the most persuasive people.

Your mindset

The first thing to realise is that, before you try and convince anyone of anything, you must be convinced yourself first. If you doubt something, the uncertainty will show up in your body, so make sure you spend time justifying to yourself why your message is spot on. You should demonstrate a feeling of certainty in what you're saying.

The emotional state you go into will have a significant impact on the people you're trying to persuade. Of course, applying what you've already learnt to put yourself in the most confident state possible is a good idea. Feeling passionate and excited is also important in most situations where you want to persuade someone of something.

On top of this, it's a good idea to think about the interaction strategically. By preparing for the various reactions you might get from the person, you put yourself in a good position to handle whatever happens in the best possible way. This means being able to feel well able to handle any situation that may arise. Since you can predict how they might react you can be prepared for this eventuality. For example, try asking these questions before meeting the other person:

How do you think about the interaction at present?

How do you feel about the interaction at present?

How would you deal with the interaction if the other person didn't respond as well as you wanted them to?

How would you feel about the interaction if the other person didn't respond well to you?

What is the most useful way to think about the interaction right now?

What is the most useful way to feel about the interaction right now?

What is the most useful way to think about a client who reacts badly to you?

What is the most useful way to feel about the interaction if it doesn't go how it's supposed to go?

The seven pillars of persuasion

Among the most prominent and repeatedly asked questions in persuasion literature are 'What kind of person is persuasive?' and

'What are the personalities and qualities the most persuasive people have?'

After examining much of the research in the field of psychology, I found that there were seven qualities in particular that seemed to be possessed by the vast majority of the most persuasive people. From Cicero to Steve Jobs, these qualities tend to be important in ensuring that the audience believes and trusts the speaker or communicator even before examining the message they're presenting.

One of the ancient experts on the topic of persuasion, Aristotle, explored these qualities in his discussion of the 'ethos' of a speaker. He regarded three qualities in particular as being important: virtue (where you share the values of the audience), wisdom and selflessness. Since then we've learnt a lot about what makes a person credible. It seems that demonstrating similarity and trustworthiness to an audience, being perceived as an expert in the subject and caring about the audience are still important attributes that anyone who wishes to influence others should possess. But other qualities, such as confidence and the ability to engage others, have also been shown to affect how credible you are.

What I want to do here is to explore each of the seven qualities that can make you come across more persuasively. I also want to explain the psychological effects relevant in each case so that you can have a clear understanding of how and why to demonstrate each characteristic. The seven qualities I refer to here are what I call the 'seven pillars of a persuasive person', and they determine how effectively the other person will listen to you and be persuaded by you.

1. Confident

As we learnt earlier, people often process their interactions with you quickly and automatically. They make swift decisions and use shortcuts or rules of thumb, known as 'heuristics', to make decisions as to whether or not the person they're listening to should be believed.

So, by means of these shortcuts we arrive at conclusions about how persuasive someone is, based on factors that aren't always connected with the actual validity or reliability of their arguments. In 2004, two researchers, Paul Price and Eric Stone, argued for the existence of a 'confidence heuristic'. It argues that people tend to believe that those who express themselves confidently are more accurate than those who don't.

So when a person communicating with us appears confident in what they're saying, we're more likely to believe them, even if we aren't sure how accurate the statements they make are. The more confident you come across, the more likely it is the other person will believe you. It's important to balance this with likeability, as you need to demonstrate that you can relate to them as well.

2. Expert

This is about how you can ensure that a client sees you as someone who knows what you're talking about. This will give them the assurance that your advice and suggestions are worth listening to. Often we look to whoever knows the most about a topic for guidance.

Now more than ever we find ourselves bombarded with an incredible amount of information. We have begun to rely more and more on experts in different areas, as we simply don't have time to study everything in much depth. When someone has got the necessary qualifications or experience, we tend to believe them when they speak.

Although confidence and expertise often go hand in hand, sometimes they don't, and it's essential that you use them both rather than rely on one or the other. If you don't feel you have the expertise in a particular topic, be clear about what expertise you do have and become an expert at knowing where to find the information they might look for.

3. Likeable

Likeability involves doing whatever you can to show respect and care for the client. The more you show them you want to help them, and that you don't want them to suffer, the more likeable you will be. So, what are the factors that make a person likeable?

The 'mere exposure' effect in psychology suggests that people tend to like other people and objects simply because they're familiar with them. Again, this cognitive bias means that likeability is affected by how many times we've met or seen someone rather by than any specific likeable trait they possess. In reality, being good to other people, and indeed many of the other charismatic actions we've discussed so far, can help you to come across as more likeable.

4. Similar

This means connecting with a client on a human level and finding ways in which you're similar to them. This could be anything from using similar words to revealing that you know what it's like to be in their position. When people feel as if you understand what it's like to be in their situation, they're more likely to trust you.

As noted in the discussion on rapport (chapter 14), from the field of NLP we have learnt that when two individuals get on well they tend to match or mirror each other's body language and way of speaking. In 1999 psychologists caught up with this idea and demonstrated it empirically, dubbing it the 'chameleon effect'. Two researchers, Tanya Chartrand and John Bargh, observed that participants in studies unconsciously matched the body language of the experimenter. They also found that when the experimenter deliberately matched the body language of the participant it had a positive effect on how much the participant liked the experimenter.

5. Engaging

When I use the term 'engaging', I'm talking about your ability to make the message easy to digest—something that stands out and that a person would find interesting or appealing. People are more persuaded when they find themselves interested in the message you're communicating.

A cognitive bias that's of interest here is known as the 'availability heuristic', a term coined by Amos Tversky and Daniel Kahneman. It suggests that when we make decisions about something, we're more likely to be persuaded by the readily available information on the subject than by the whole set of data on it. When you use examples that are easy to imagine, vivid and memorable, the other person finds it easier to bring them to mind, which, in turn, makes them more available. So when you make a point that involves a memorable and powerful story, people are more likely to think of the story than about the rest of what you might have said.

One way to be more engaging is to say something that goes against the norm or is counterintuitive. The 'isolation effect' suggests that we're far more likely to remember something unusual than anything perceived as normal.

So the key to being engaging is to make yourself relevant, memorable and vivid, and to stand out as different or unusual.

6. Trustworthy

It's important to be as transparent as possible when speaking to someone. If you lie to them, or even mislead them, you'll find it next to impossible to have them ever listen to you again. The bottom line is that coming across as open and honest is best achieved by *being* open and honest. Trust is built largely by being trustworthy. However, this doesn't mean that you simply avoid lying: it also means that whenever you promise to do something for someone you actually follow through and do it when you said you were going to do it.

For example, a few years ago I worked with a call centre that made cold calls to businesses. They had a problem in that they didn't get the chance to pitch their business to the key contact before being cut off. What I got them to do was to make an adjustment to what they said at the beginning of the call. As soon as the contact answered the phone the representative would say something along the lines of:

> Hello, sir. My name is . . . from . . . I believe we can help you to . . . I wonder if you could give me exactly sixty seconds of your time to explain how. If after sixty seconds you don't want to hear any more I promise we'll finish the call and I'll never bother you again. Can you give me sixty seconds?

The key, though, was what they did next. I instructed the representatives that at that point they were to start a stopwatch and begin the pitch. After exactly a minute, even if they were in the middle of a sentence, they were to interrupt themselves and say:

> I've noticed that the sixty seconds I asked for have expired. I'd love to tell you more if you have more time, but if not that's okay too, as you've given me the time I asked for. Would you like to hear more?

This had a huge impact on how well they did. Not only did they get to make their pitch, but the pitch was more successful. By saying they would do something and then following through on it, even at the cost of the pitch, they built massive trust and credibility with the other person.

Every time you say you're going to do something and then do it when you said you were going to do it, you build trust in the mind of another person. Every time you fail to do so, even if they don't notice the discrepancy consciously, they still have the experience of you not being true to your word. This eats away at your perceived credibility.

7. Open

When we talk to someone, there is in most cases something we want to get out of the interaction. Maybe it's a sale, a date, an agreement or a better relationship. Regardless, one of the really important things to do is to ensure that you're open about what it is you want, and to do your best to get the other person to be open about what they want.

One of the most important lessons I learnt from studying strategic negotiation at Harvard Business School was the idea of always probing for the shared interests that lie behind the positions people hold in any negotiation. James Sibenius, our professor for the course, discussed the importance of uncovering these values. Instead of assuming that both parties will have to make big sacrifices, the idea is that they often have different interests. If both parties are open about what they want, rather than sticking to their positions, you can find better solutions.

For example, in 1979, Israel and Egypt—which had been in a state of constant war with each other since 1948—finally arrived at a peaceful settlement. They had been in conflict over the ownership of the Sinai Peninsula, which Israel had captured during the 1967 war. The two sides finally came to a resolution by being open about their agendas. The Israelis said they wanted ownership of it because of security concerns. The Egyptians, on the other hand, wanted to retain ownership because of the historical significance of the region. Because of this, the deal they agreed included the following compromise: Egypt would get back the territory if they promised to leave it as a completely demilitarised zone.

So, when you want to influence someone, being open about what you want, and being interested in finding a way to help get the other person what they want, can help ensure that they will trust you more. Since they know you have an agenda, when you're forthcoming about it they see that you're not hiding anything, and so you're perceived as being more truthful. Also, as we can see from the negotiation examples, being straight up about what you really want can help you come to better agreements when working with others.

The key to using the seven pillars in influencing others is to treat them as a sort of checklist. Every time you go into an interaction in which you want to persuade the other person, ask yourself the question, 'How am I demonstrating those seven qualities when I'm communicating with them?'

THE 'SEVEN PILLARS' EXERCISE
Ask yourself the following questions before any interaction:

1. Confidence
How will you demonstrate confidence in communicating with your audience?

_____

_____

_____

_____

_____

_____

2. Expertise
How will you demonstrate your expertise in communicating with your audience?

_____

_____

_____

_____

_____

_____

3. Likeability
How will you become more likeable in communicating with your audience?

_____

_____

_____

_____

_____

_____

4. Similarity

How will you demonstrate similarity in communicating with your audience?

_____

_____

_____

_____

_____

_____

5. Engagement

How will you be more engaging in communicating with your audience?

_____

_____

_____

_____

_____

_____

6. Trust

How will you build trust in communicating with your audience?

_____

_____

_____

_____

_____

_____

7. Openness

How will you be open about what you want and demonstrate that you want to help them get what they want?

_____

_____

_____

_____

_____

THE MESSAGE (WHAT YOU WANT THEM TO BELIEVE, DO, FEEL)
I have a number of messages in this book. In order to influence you to believe these messages, I have to pay attention to how I present them. For example, psychological research suggests that there are two main routes of persuasion. The central route is to try to persuade using logic. Some people will process the information thoughtfully, requiring effective, intelligent arguments that use language patterns. (For example an advertisement stating that studies have shown that their toothpaste is better.)

The other route is the peripheral route. This is when a person attempts to persuade using emotion and feeling. Some people will process the information effortlessly and simply, making a link between the information and a good feeling. (For example an advertisement that shows a beautiful model using toothpaste.)

Now, most people tend to be persuaded by the peripheral route, except when they're thinking about important decisions that require a lot of analysis. But the greatest persuasive messages are those that incorporate both emotional and logical means to influence others.

Emotional influence

Emotional influence is about getting the person to feel really good about you and your message; it's about having them feel desire for your product or service; it's about having them feel motivated and inspired by your brand. So what are the keys to influencing others?

The first thing to know when working on the emotional content of a message is both the emotions the other person may already be feeling and the ones you want them to be feeling. The three questions that must be answered are:

What emotions will the other person be feeling?
What emotions do you want them to be feeling?
What strategies can you use to change their feelings?

People often make decisions that are based on how they feel. They then justify the decisions using logic. This shows just how important feelings actually are in decision-making and in influence scenarios.

Examples of the kinds of emotion that are useful to create when you're trying to influence other people include interest, fascination, motivation, excitement, determination, belief, love, hope, inspiration, curiosity, openness, awareness and fun.

When people are curious or open they're more likely to take in the message effectively. When they're having fun, feel hopeful or are fascinated by something, they're more likely to associate positive qualities with the message. When they're motivated or inspired they're more likely to act on a message.

Fear is one example of a negative emotion that's used quite often in persuasive attempts. Marketing experts and political strategists, instead of focusing on the positive feelings for choosing their product or candidate, will warn against buying or voting for the other option. They use fear because fear grabs attention, and, from a psychological point of view, people do whatever they can to avoid danger.

Strategies of emotional influence

The strategies you can use to change another person's emotion involve many of the skills and tactics we examined in part 2 and some of the skills you'll learn later in this part. I've outlined seven strategies you can use to get the person you're talking to into a better state.

1. Your state

Whatever you're feeling will be transmitted to the other person. Whatever state you want them to be in, go into it yourself first and you will find yourself.

What do you want them to feel? How can you start feeling that feeling now?

2. Their physiology

The physiology of your audience will determine how they feel at an emotional level as well. If you want to keep your audience focused and in a receptive learning state (during a presentation, for example), it makes sense to have them stand up and stretch every forty-five minutes or so and to get them to access physical postures associated with learning and energy.

What can you do that gets the person into a more useful physiological state?

3. Rapport

The more you get on with someone, the more they will feel good around you. The more they feel good around you, the more they will feel good about your message.

How can you match and mirror a person to create a connection with them during the interaction?

4. Questions

Questions determine what a person will focus on. One of my favourite things to do when I meet a couple who are arguing is to ask them how they met. As soon as they start answering the question, they light up and access the feelings they had back then. Questions can be extremely effective.

So, what questions can you ask that will get the person into a positive state and make them feel good?

5. Compliments and praise

Say nice things to people, genuinely, and you will make them feel good. People respond well to encouragement and praise.

How can you compliment, encourage or praise the other person to make them feel good?

6. Stories

One of the primary functions of storytelling is that stories create emotions. As you will learn in the chapter on storytelling (chapter 21), you can impact the emotions of your audience with a well-crafted and well-told story. We read books and go to the cinema and theatre to be affected emotionally. It's the stories we experience that do that so effectively.

What stories can you tell that make the other person feel a particularly good feeling?

7. Humour

Making someone laugh is one of the best ways to help them access a good emotional state. When we laugh and feel good we're more receptive to ideas and suggestions.

How can you make the other person laugh?

Logical influence

Since we're supposed to be logical creatures, most people try and focus on improving their ability to use logic when they want to convince someone of something. As you've learnt, we vastly overrate our tendency to use logic when evaluating a message. Emotional influence trumps logic more often than not. Nonetheless, logic is still important in many contexts. There are two language patterns in particular that help you present a message in a more logically compelling way: truisms and presuppositions.

TRUISMS

Truisms, for our purposes, are true statements or comments that are accepted automatically by another person as being accurate. They're often common-sense facts you can use to build credibility. When they're used in sales, they can sometimes result in getting people to say 'yes' a number of times in a row (known as 'yes-yes sets'). To use them, simply state something you know will be true for the client. When you do this, the client will be agreeing with you in their mind, and that will position you as being more credible.

So, for example, if you want to win over a client to use your phone network, you could start by saying a number of things you know they will agree with.

There are many different kinds of phone out there, and you obviously want one that works for you whenever you need it to. Of course, it's not just the phone but the quality of the network you use. Again, you have a number of different choices here. But whatever choice you make it's essential that this network works for you in an efficient and reliable manner. Dropping calls would be completely unacceptable. You need a network you can count on.

The salesperson has by this time said seven statements the client will certainly be thinking 'yes' to. So this is a really great way to build credibility with the client.

PRESUPPOSITIONS

Presuppositions are when you assume something to be true. They're very powerful ways to indirectly influence other people. You can do so by assuming certain things to be true as you state them and thus linguistically create certain 'truths' without needing to back them up with evidence.

There are many different types of presuppositions. Some are related to time. So, for example, when talking about a period before something is happening you can presuppose that the event will happen. The following are six types of presupposition:

Time-based presuppositions (*before, during, after, while, begin,* *start, continue, end*): By positioning something in time you presuppose that it will happen. For example, when talking about 'before' something is happening you presuppose that the event will happen.

Order-based presuppositions (*first, second, another*): By positioning an item in an order, you presuppose that other elements exist. For example, when you say 'the third thing' it presupposes that there's a first and second.

'Or' presuppositions: This is when you give the person two options, yet both work in your favour ('Would you like to pay by cash or credit card?'). This presupposes that they will pay.

Awareness presuppositions (*realise, become aware of, understand, notice, discover*): This is when you discuss the awareness of something. By discussing it you presuppose that it exists. For example, if you say, 'Do you realise that this is the best course of action?' you presuppose that it's the best course of action. The question is whether you've realised it yet or not.

Descriptive presuppositions (*how easily, how quickly, how effectively*): An example of this is when you ask, 'How easy would you find this to do?' By putting it that way you presuppose that it will be easy. The question is 'How easy?'

Commentary presuppositions (*fortunately, obviously, luckily, clearly*): This is when you make a comment about something and, by the fact of making it, presuppose that it is the state of affairs. (For example: 'Unfortunately, this is our only available course of action.') This presupposes that it's your only available course of action.

So, after you've decided that it's a really great idea, and before you start to use presuppositions effectively, first practise them whenever you get a chance and then use them to help you influence others.

Another reason to practise presuppositions is that—whether you notice yourself doing it all the time, or even most of the time, and whether or not it's easy or simple, fun or enjoyable—you'll realise that you can become better at influencing others. You'll discover that you already use presuppositions in language, and you'll become aware of how you can deliberately use them to get your desired result. I'm not sure how easy you'll find it or how quickly you'll become more effective; but, fortunately, the more you practise, the better you'll get. And, obviously, you have a lot of opportunities to practise! This paragraph was particularly persuasive, because I'm not 'telling' you something: I'm 'assuming' something, which makes it sound far more valid.

Two-sided message

Some of the best messages anticipate the issues or problems the other person might have with what you're telling them. These messages include both sides of the argument but explain how one side (the side they propose) far outweighs the other. This can be very powerful, as the other person will find it harder to argue the opposing argument, because you've already defended yourself against it.

MEDIUM (HOW IS THE MESSAGE TO BE DELIVERED?)

When I visited North Korea, I was given an incredible insight into how propaganda works. What I realised was that many of the things used there aren't all that different from what we experience in the West. Often it's just that we're much more subtle about it. The key is in exploring how you can prepare to use whatever format you have to present your message in the best possible way.

The medium of any message is the channel in which you present it. Whereas the 'how' refers to the emotional and rational appeals you use, the medium is about 'how it is presented'. There are two elements in working effectively with the medium for your message: format and framing.

Format

The first aspect to consider when looking at the medium of your message is the atmosphere in which the message will be delivered. Will the person be in a large auditorium? At home in their living room? Listening to the radio at home or in their car? In conversation in person? The answers will be determined by how you best set up the medium.

For example, if you ever watch a presentation by Steve Jobs telling the world about a new Apple product, you'll notice that there's great detail in the background. The way the presentation is set up is perfect for the audience—where the cameras are pointing, the size of each shot. In fact, my colleague Alessio Roberti once pointed out that even the typeface Jobs uses on his slides correspond to the words. For instance, when he was explaining the Macbook Air the word 'air' was written in a very thin and light typeface, which added to the impact of the word.

But the environment can be altered by the other senses as well. For instance, I went to the cinema in Japan when I was working over there recently, and the smell of sweet popcorn was so powerful that I found myself unable to resist the temptation to buy it (it was the smell, not gluttony—honest!).

Then there's the use of sound. Some supermarkets tend to play faster music during busy periods (when they want people to buy more quickly) and slower music at quieter times (when they'd prefer people to go more slowly and to engage more in impulse buying). Of course, impulse buying is also improved by placing sweet treats at the cash register, within easy reach. As people have their money out already, it's a prime time for pouncing on their unsuspecting sugar cravings.

If you're preparing for a short radio or television interview, the key is to get some sound bites ready and aim to grab the audience's interest without going into great detail. On the other hand, if you're being interviewed for an article or a book you can go into more detail. On radio you'll have to ensure that your voice is at its best. And on television, of course, you'll need to look your best. When speaking to a big crowd you should do your best to have a large image of your logo behind you and, if possible, large screens with a close-up of you. The key is to have every part of the background conveying the same message to the audience. For business presentations a slick-looking slideshow can help present you in an engaging way.

The main question here is: how can you use the specific medium you will be presented in as best you can?

Framing

The concept of framing is also important in the medium in which you present your message. Framing describes how you present an idea. The difference between something being educational and it being propaganda is how it's framed. In fact, many would suggest that there's no such thing as 'being free from bias' and that everything is framed in some way.

When you first speak on a certain topic, your opening remarks will frame what you're focusing on, so make sure the first few sentences make clear what your message is. In this context, the psychological principle of 'priming' occurs when you affect how people process a message by means of what you've said to them before that message. So, for example, if you say that something is good news before you say what it is, people are more likely to look for the good in it than if you primed the news by saying it would be bad news. People look for what they expect, so get them to expect what you want.

The key question here is: how can you frame things so that you position yourself in the best possible way and make it more likely that people will believe you?

AUDIENCE (WHO IS THE MESSAGE FOR?)

The most influential people in the world don't just position themselves as highly credible and prepare their message emotionally and logically in the appropriate medium: they also understand who they're talking to. There's a massive amount that can be learnt from paying attention to the person you're trying to influence. You've already learnt some examples of how you can do this in the chapter on reading other people (chapter 13).

The key with persuading people is to find out what they want, believe, fear and value. Once you do this the next step is to understand any psychological factors that might influence their decisions.

1. How much have you researched the audience in relation to who they are and what they want, value, fear and believe?

2. What psychological factors are at play?

Audience research

To influence people as effectively as possible, it's vital to do your homework on the audience you're trying to persuade. Some of the most successful marketing firms on the planet emphasise the importance of finding out as much information as you can about your audience. You need to take some time to ask a number of questions so that you're clear about how you want to communicate with them for the best possible result.

Who are they?
Who do they see themselves as?
Who do they want to be?
What do they want?
How, when and why do they want it?
What is important to them?
What do they need?
What do they fear?

What do they believe or think about you?
What might they think or believe about your message?
What might they think or believe about themselves in relation to the message?
What key words are important for them?

Answering these questions will help you understand how to strategically present your message in the best possible way in order to get them to believe it.

Psychological factors

There are a number of psychological principles that can help you to understand how an audience will respond to the message you present to them. Robert Cialdini is a well-known researcher who classified six principles of persuasion. Understanding these principles can help you to improve how you influence others.

1. Commitment

When you commit to something it's much easier to be persuaded to keep with that commitment. The 'foot-in-the-door phenomenon', as it's called, is where we're more likely to be persuaded by someone to do something big once they've got us to do something small.

2. Reciprocation

When someone does something for you, you're much more likely to feel obliged to do something for them.

3. Liking

When you like someone they're more likely to persuade you. We've already examined this as one of the seven pillars of a persuasive person.

4. Authority

When you respect someone for knowing more about something than you they're much more likely to persuade you. This is similar to the pillar of expertise, discussed as a quality of the most persuasive you.

5. Scarcity

When it's really hard to get something, you want it that much more.

6. Social proof

You're more likely to conform to some kind of influence if others have conformed first. The 'bandwagon effect' is a well-documented form of groupthink in behavioural science and has many applications. The general rule is that conduct or beliefs spread among people, as fads and trends clearly do, with 'the probability of any individual adopting it increasing with the proportion who have already done so.'

For more information on these, see Cialdini's book *Influence: The Psychology of Persuasion*, which is well known and well worth reading.

THE 'PRINCIPLES OF INFLUENCE' EXERCISE

Here are some questions to ask yourself in order to apply Cialdini's principles.

How can you get a small commitment from the person first?

_____

_____

_____

_____

_____

_____

What can you give the other person first to create a feeling of reciprocity?

_____

_____

_____

_____

_____

How can you become more likeable?

_____

_____

_____

_____

_____

How can you demonstrate authority?

_____

_____

_____

_____

_____

_____

How can you make your product or service seem more scarce and therefore valuable?

_____

_____

_____

_____

_____

_____

How can you make your product, service or message appear really popular?

_____

_____

_____

_____

_____

_____

Chapter 20
How to make people laugh

Tragedy is when I cut my finger. Comedy is when you fall into an open sewer and die.

MEL BROOKS

A few years ago, I was in Bangalore in India teaching a number of NLP workshops. A friend of mine, Rob, came over to visit me during a couple of my days off, and we fitted in a packed schedule of adventures. One thing we managed to do was to organise a very special spiritual reading by a local guru. We arrived about midday in the ashram. A friend of mine from India, Harry, was looking after us, and he led us into the private room in the back. There was a strong smell of incense, and Rob and I took our seats on one side of the table as we waited for the guru to arrive. We had been told that this experience was very special, so we kept silent out of respect as soon as we entered the room. The only sound was the clock on the wall, with its metronomic ticking. After a few minutes, the door opened and an old Indian man glided in.

We instinctively stood and bowed to greet him as he made his way to his chair. He began to speak about the process. The guru spoke in soft whispers, every word beaming with enlightenment. We were transfixed, completely absorbed as we were led on this special spiritual journey.

After a few minutes of these words of wisdom the guru closed his eyes and began to connect with a higher power. His head rocked back and forth and from side to side as he made a number of strange sounds. Rob and I sat still, aware that something magical was happening. This was the key moment. The guru opened his eyes. We held our breath.

At that exact moment the door burst open. Harry's smiling face appeared, and, oblivious to what was going on, he loudly informed us that he was going for pizzas and asked us what kind we wanted. Instinctively we went red, embarrassed that this sacred process had been interrupted. After we blurted out very quick responses, the embarrassment gave way to nervous laughter, and the two of us pressed our lips shut, attempting to hold it in. The door closed and we were left alone once more with the guru.

Once again he spoke for a minute or so in his magical tone of voice, before closing his eyes and letting his head rock back and forth and from side to side in the same ritual as before. The metronome of the clock filled the silence. Again, this was the key moment. He opened his eyes and began to speak.

But, once again, Harry burst into the room. 'Do you want Coke, 7 Up, Fanta, Diet Coke?' he asked loudly, his big face smiling.

This was too much. As we again answered quickly, Harry didn't seem to notice and stayed standing in the doorway while he slowly read us back the order.

'So, that's two plain tomato and cheese pizzas, one Sprite and one Diet Coke?'

'Yes,' we replied hurriedly.

'Okay. And do you want any garlic bread with that?'

'No.'

With that, Harry once again closed the door. As the guru yet again began his process, Rob and I fought as hard as we could not to laugh.

You know that feeling when you're trying really, really hard not to burst out laughing? When your stomach is shaking and you're pursing your lips tightly together? When you feel your face flushed and the corners or your mouth pressing themselves upwards?

Well, as we sat there waiting for the guru's pearls of wisdom, Rob and I did all we could not to look at each other. In my peripheral vision, I could see him shaking, trying desperately to keep the laughter in; it made me shake more, which made him shake more. We tried to raise our hands to cover our faces, but it was no use.

Finally, as the guru opened his eyes and spoke, we both burst out laughing. We couldn't stop. Tears came as we broke down in convulsions, holding our stomachs in a desperate attempt to regain some composure. Luckily for us, as the puzzled guru looked at us, curious about what we were laughing at, he too started laughing, and the three of us continued, unable to speak for at least five minutes. Every time we tried we broke down again.

Times like these stick out in my memory because of the fun we had. You see, you tend to remember the funniest experiences you've ever had. You tend to remember the funniest people you've ever met. They make a powerful impression on you—one that lasts a long time in your memory.

When I was studying psychology, one of the subjects I examined was comedy. A project I did focused on two comedians, Billy Connolly and Eddie Izzard. I explored and examined how they both made people laugh and conducted an analysis of their performances.

Watching the videos was hilarious, and analysing how they did what they did was fascinating. But the process of examining the theories of humour was absolute torture. I trawled through study after study on comedy and the science of humour. It really is possible to make anything boring if you work at it.

So in explaining 'how to make people laugh', I'm not going to spend much time at all talking to you about theories of humour. Instead, I want to explore as many ways as I can to actually 'be funny'.

Many people reading this, I know, may well be thinking, Is it not fair to say that some people are just naturally funny and others are not? Well, like charismatic individuals, there are some people who seem to be more naturally charismatic, but we all have the capacity to improve how funny we are. You can see that many stand-up comedians become funnier over time. This suggests that it's possible to become funnier. Learning about the different strategies of humour, as well as about core skills such as timing and expression, can help you make people laugh more.

Because I travel around the world, I spend a lot of time on planes, trains and taxis. I spend a lot of time on my own. A *lot* of time. In 2012, I travelled on more than a hundred flights, and on the vast majority of these I was alone. I spent more than a hundred and fifty days in a strange bed in a foreign hotel, often going for dinner by myself in a local restaurant. It's critical that I enjoy my own company. I do. Why? Well, quite frankly, I'm hilarious. Not necessarily to other people, but to myself. I laugh at my own jokes a lot and have hours of fun with my own thoughts. Now, I know that's strange. Sometimes I'll randomly laugh when I'm in a public place because of a particular thought I have.

Now, before you raise an eyebrow and consider the possibility that I need psychological attention, think about anything you find funny.

In order to share it with others, you must first find it funny yourself. Becoming better at making people laugh must begin with the way you think about the world. That means, once again, returning to the importance of attitude. Before becoming funnier you must learn to think in a funnier way, and from that place you'll find yourself making others laugh more as well.

Humour is an essential element of charisma. When you can make people laugh you're already powerfully affecting their opinion of you. There are a number of factors involved in developing your ability to be humorous. Firstly, it's important to be aware of some of the different types of humour. Secondly, there's the funniest frame of mind to be in. Thirdly, there's what moods help you to be at your comical best. Finally, there are the actual core techniques and habits for using humour effectively.

TYPES OF HUMOUR
There are many different types of humour. I want to talk about just four: ambiguities, story humour, observational comedy and presentational comedy.

Ambiguities
Ambiguities are often described as the backbone of humour. When you're laughing it's often funny because a joke has revealed a meaning different from what you expected at the start. Jokes usually contain a word or phrase that has a double meaning, and it's the resolution of this meaning that makes people laugh. For example: 'A giraffe walks into a bar, and the barman says, "Why the long face?"' The 'long face' is literally true about the animal's features, but it's also an expression meaning to feel sad.

Practise paying attention to ambiguities, listening for them and writing them down. This will hone efficiency in your brain and enable you to develop your linguistic skills more powerfully.

Story humour
Story humour is an important type of humour, used mainly by comedians, that involves telling a story in the most amusing way possible. It's a good exercise to go back through your life and to note the funniest stories and experiences you've ever had. Then practise telling them and make whatever changes are necessary to make the

story funnier. Remember to practise ways of enhancing the story for the listener: be more expressive, practise accents (which are often funny) and so on.

Remember, however, that story humour works not because of the amusing incidents in themselves but because of the way you recount the story. So, you can make anything funny. When something funny happens many people think that when they describe it to others they will automatically find it funny too. The common expression 'I guess you had to be there' is evidence of the fact that stories often don't work, even if they seem hilarious to the person describing them.

Observational comedy

Observational comedy is the type of humour where comedians talk about the real world and point out all the hilarious things that can be found in it. They might draw attention to the more ridiculous laws of a country, to the stupid things a person has said or to crazy ideas that people have.

The trick, however, is that it's only because of the way such things are described, and because of the connections that are made, that you realise just how funny it all actually is. Before you were made aware of the humour of it you might have observed the situation neutrally, but it's the comedian who made it funny.

Presentational comedy

Presentational comedy is humour that's funny because something is presented in a very funny way. For example, many comedians are excellent at impersonating people or putting on accents, and when they do so it's very funny to hear. When someone pokes fun at others their ability to observe the quirkiness of the other person, together with their ability to impersonate them, will determine how funny they are.

Presentational comedy is all about how you use your face, body, voice and words to present ideas in the funniest way. Sometimes you don't even need words: Laurel and Hardy and Charlie Chaplin are good examples of pure presentational comedy.

THE COMEDY MINDSET

In order to be funny, it's essential that you learn to look at the world in a funny way. Watch lots of comedians and funny programmes and you will notice that most of the things you find funny are not, in and of themselves, funny. Instead, they're funny because of the way in which they're presented. So to improve your sense of humour and your ability to make people laugh, the first step is to get yourself to understand the truth about humour.

Humour is about taking situations and looking at them from another point of view. It's about flexibility: the more you can creatively look at things in different ways, the more humorous you will become. Everyone has the potential to be funny. There's no such thing as a 'humour gene' that some people don't have. Even if some people do it more naturally (like golf, like charisma), we all have the ability to do it pretty well. The more you're exposed to humour, the more you will begin to develop a funny way of looking at the world, because being funny is something you can learn. The more you practise, the better you will get.

Find it funny first and you'll find it easier to make it funny.

THE 'LAUGHTER FILTER' EXERCISE

This exercise is a very effective method of dealing with problems. Often it's our negative response to the world that impacts on us in a non-useful way. Many comedians use this strategy in order to be funny. The key topics are things that are weird, difficult or annoying, or things you hate, make you angry or make you worried. Take the situation or problem you're thinking about and ask yourself the question, 'How would a stand-up comedian describe this experience?' The types of humour and the tips mentioned above are some examples of what devices to use to help develop your laughter filter. Watch plenty of stand-up comedians and ask yourself the question, 'How do they see the world?' By asking that question you will find yourself naturally seeing the funny side of your problems and enjoying this fun process.

THE COMEDY MOOD

It's also important to be in the most useful states in order for you to get other people laughing. Here are some things I've found that really help.

Confidence

Confidence is useful in order for you to present yourself to others in a way that makes people laugh. If people think you're nervous they won't be as receptive to you making them laugh.

Playfulness
Playfulness is a key state in making people laugh. You have to be in a state where you're playing with ideas in a fun way, as that's the best state in which to present things in the funniest way possible.

Expressiveness
Expressiveness means being in a state where you're fully expressing how you feel. To impact other people, you need to physically show how you're thinking or feeling in as vivid a way as possible. The more facial expressions you can use, the more flexible you will be in making everything you say more animated and therefore funnier.

Creativity
Creativity is the state where you actively come up with new ways to look at and think about things. The more creative you are, the more choices you have as to what kind of humour you present.

Outrageousness
Often, the more outrageous a state you're in, the more effective you will be at getting other people's states to be affected by you, and, therefore, the more likely it is you will get them to laugh.

COMEDY TECHNIQUES
There are a number of useful techniques you can practise and develop to become funnier in different styles of humour.

Pullback and reveal
My friend and top Irish comedian, Karl Spain, explained to me that the vast majority of jokes involve a set-up, where you begin the joke, and a punchline, where you hit them (metaphorically speaking!) with the funny twist. He calls this 'pullback and reveal'. You hold the punchline for as long as possible, so that the end of the joke becomes much more powerful. For example: 'There used to be a Statoil down the road from me, but now it's just a shell.' In this case, the entire joke is contained in the very last word, which is an ambiguity that could refer either to something that's small or to the company Shell. By

making the punchline shorter and placing it at the very end of the sentence, you can make it all the more effective.

Callback

Callback happens whenever you take a funny idea that has already produced laughter and you link it to something new you're talking about. In this way the earlier idea becomes even funnier, and it also makes whatever you're talking about now even funnier.

There's a wonderful example of callback in Eddie Izzard's stand-up performance 'Glorious', when he mimics a baboon making a particular sound. Half an hour later, another mime, sawing a plank of wood, involves a sound effect that allows him to say, 'And soon he realised he was punching a baboon.' In this way he brought the previous mime into the present one, and the audience laughed at both the new one and the memory of the earlier one. A callback borrows laughter from the past and adds it to the present.

Satire

When I was working on 'Not Enough Hours', as a joke I recorded a seven-minute satire of it in which I made fun of myself. Since I used a catchphrase throughout the programme, 'Does that make sense?', the satirical character (who was also played by me) kept repeating that phrase. In the skit, I turned up late and kept losing my focus (despite the fact that I was supposed to be helping people to become more focused and punctual), and I also kept bringing every problem back to the recession and blaming it on that (which was the theme of some of our shows). I never released the satire, but any of the crew I showed it to, and all my friends, thought it was hilarious. It turns out I'm pretty good at knowing how ridiculous I seem.

Satire is a good skill to master. It involves making fun of a particular thing by exaggerating the ridiculousness of it. Ask yourself the question, 'How can I satirise this situation or experience?' Doing this involves you finding out what's ridiculous about something and exaggerating it. To watch this in action check out the comedy series 'The Office', which satirises the boss of a paper company.

Sarcasm

Sarcasm is a great form of humour in which you say the opposite of what you mean but in such a way that others know you don't mean it.

For example, let's say you're cleaning the car and someone comes over and asks, 'What are you doing, cleaning the car?' You could respond, 'No, I'm not cleaning the car, I'm inventing space and time while simultaneously learning to play the piano.'

Once, when I was teaching a seminar in Okinawa, I got second-degree burns on both legs as a result of sunburn (I fell asleep on the beach), and I was confined to a wheelchair for a few days. At one stage when I was teaching, someone asked, 'Oh, did you hurt yourself?' to which I replied, 'No, it was actually quite pleasant. I woke up one morning with sunburn on both legs and just decided it would be fun to sit down for a few days.'

Of course, it's important to judge the situation. A cheeky smile is necessary, as sarcasm can sometimes offend people and come across as mean. So, gauge your audience. But it's still pretty funny when used properly. Ask yourself the question, 'In what way can I be sarcastic about my experiences and the situation I find myself in?'

Exaggeration

Exaggeration is a great way to make anything funny. Most things are hilarious when you take them to their extreme. Ask yourself the following questions: 'How can I exaggerate my story and the elements of my story to make it ridiculous?' and 'How can I use more extreme language and generalisations to make the situation funnier?'

One good trick is to think of a particular attribute like 'smart', 'tall' or 'strong' and make a list of persons, places and things that are examples of extreme cases of each attribute. Once you do this you'll have plenty of opportunities to exaggerate when speaking about that attribute.

So, for example, instead of saying, 'He was very stupid,' you could say, 'He was so stupid he studied for a drug test.' Or in the place of 'She was small' you could say, 'She was so small you could see her feet on her driving licence.'

Reality violations

When you ascribe a quality to an object or thing that doesn't normally have that quality, it can often have hilarious results. For example, you can attribute human qualities to other species or to inanimate objects. It's a lot easier to make fun of things if we imagine what it would be like if dogs or cats were in our position, and what they would think and do or how they would react. (In literature this is known as anthropomorphism, and by the term 'reality violations'.)

One of the classic examples of this is a stand-up routine by Billy Connolly in which he acts out what he saw in a wildlife documentary when lions attacked wildebeests. Billy plays both parts in a hilarious sketch—it's comedy gold. Another example is when Richard Pryor goes hunting in 'Live in Concert'. Eddie Izzard's giraffe sketch and computer sketch in 'Glorious' are pretty good as well. You can find all these on YouTube.

COMEDY HABITS
Here are some good habits to practise regularly.

Sourcing material
Sourcing good material from your own life is a great skill in and of itself. The key is to search for things in your life, that you see on television or hear of somewhere else in the world that are credible and strange and yet real. Often the best humour comes from saying things that no-one ever says but that everyone thinks. By describing this truth you can get a great response. You can use things that annoy you, disgust you or anger you. All are good topics for humour.

Using gestural language
Watch great mime artists. Using only gestures, they're able to convey ideas brilliantly. It's worth practising games like charades to refine your ability to convey information with your body language. Often it's by presenting ideas visually that you're at your funniest.

Timing
Timing is obviously important, though there are a couple of things to bear in mind about it. Firstly, it's important to present the set-up, then pause, before presenting the punchline in as succinct a way as possible. The pause should always come just before you make it funny. Secondly, it's useful to remember that things often sound better and funnier when you use groups of three. For some reason, whenever you make comparisons it's easier to get people laughing if you present the ideas in such a group (A, B and C).

This is the source of all 'an Englishman, an Irishman and a Scotsman' jokes, which have a number of cultural variations in different parts of the world. For example, in Poland they say, 'A Pole, a German and a Russian', and in Russia 'A Russian, an American and a German'.

Expressiveness

Once you're in the right kind of state with the right attitude, the next step is to ensure that you use your face, body and tone of voice as best you can. It's critical that you develop a good flexibility in the way you speak, as your tone of voice enables you to perform many of the functions required for being funny. Impersonating accents, saying something sarcastically, making funny noises—all these require you to have good control over the range of sounds you can make using your tone of voice.

Similarly, the way you express yourself facially should be very much exaggerated, especially when speaking to a large group of people. When you communicate to others, the state you're in is often visible on your face, so the more you practise making your 'tone of face' exaggerated, the more you'll infect them with how you feel.

Your use of body language and the way you hold yourself are also important, and you can practise describing jokes, funny stories and observations by using your face and voice, as well as your whole body. You will find yourself getting much better responses as a result.

Observational skills

If you pay attention to the world in detail, you will find cases of ridiculousness that you can talk about. Ask yourself the question, 'How can I pay attention to the literal use of language and notice the ridiculous behaviour people engage in during the unfolding of my problem situation?'

For example, a great Australian comedian, Adam Hills, has a terrific sketch about Irish people and our use of spatial language. He cites various examples, such as the phrase 'Go on', which we use to get a person to keep talking to us, and 'Go away', which we use to express surprise about what a person tells us. It's because he's from outside Ireland that he was able to notice these expressions and the amusing difference between their meaning to Irish people and their meaning to someone else.

Practice in the real world

The key with all these skills is to practise them over and over again both by yourself and when you're with others. Humour is something that requires feedback in order to help you improve. You will learn the art of effective timing by telling the same joke or funny story in different ways. Always pay attention to which parts of your story people find funniest and laugh at most, and to which versions tend to get the best response. Become a student of humour and you'll soon master the fine art of being funnier.

Chapter 21

How to tell a captivating story

The universe is made of stories, not atoms.

MURIEL RUKEYSER

Picture this. It's 200,000 BC. You are a *Homo sapiens* (HS) living in the heart of Africa. You are about to go to hunt for some food. You leave your shelter and begin the long walk through the jungle. On your way you meet a fellow-HS (of course, you don't know that you're called that!) and he has bite marks across his chest and is walking with a limp. The conversation goes like this:

> 'All right, head, what happened to you?'
> 'Hey, pal, not a good day all round. I tell you, there are lots of lions lying around about two miles up. I went there and they bleedin' savaged me! If I were you, I'd steer well clear of that and go east instead.'
> 'Thanks, buddy!'

Okay, maybe the conversation wouldn't go exactly like that, but there would be sounds exchanged and plenty of gestures, and they would warn you off. You would have just heard a story . . . and that story might just have saved your life!

Stories have been used since the dawn of language to transfer information from person to person. The ability to share experiences is something that has proved invaluable to our capacity to learn and improve. At first this was done orally, but after the invention of writing and alphabets, people began to write stories down.

The most popular book of all time is the Bible. Along with a number of other religious texts from different societies, it makes up one big story. These stories have helped guide entire ways of life for millions of people. The power of stories is apparent everywhere. From

Hollywood to Bollywood, television and cinema screens throughout the world present us with story after story, and we find ourselves easily drawn into them.

The reason stories are so popular is that we're actually hard-wired to respond powerfully to them. Lisa Cron, in her fascinating book *Wired for Story*, explains that our brains release a feel-good chemical called dopamine when we're paying attention to a story, in anticipation of what happens next. We're biologically wired to enjoy hearing stories, because, as we evolved, stories provided us with valuable information about how to learn from other people's experience. They told us what to do and how to handle new challenges, and therefore our brains kept rewarding us because of the positive benefits they provided for our chances of survival.

The connection between charisma and storytelling is an interesting one. When you communicate with others, a large part of what you say will involve stories. When we tell a person what we've done or what we're going to do, we usually use stories. Your ability to master the craft of storytelling is connected to how well you can entice and interest the other person.

So, in this chapter, I want to explore the functions of storytelling—the reasons people tell stories. In other words, how can you best think about the storytelling process in order to become more interesting to listen to? I also want to examine the core skills necessary for actually grabbing (and keeping) people's attention with the stories you tell them. What are the secrets that novelists and screenwriters know about for telling stories that can help you be able to influence the people you talk to?

THE FUNCTIONS OF STORYTELLING

Although many people see stories as a way of sharing experiences with another person, there are a number of other things they allow you to do. Some find themselves telling stories without really exploring why they're telling them. By understanding the function of storytelling, you can ensure that you maximise your ability to affect people. So, what are the four main functions of storytelling?

1. To share experiences: We grow up learning to tell stories so that we can share information, opinions and, most importantly, experiences with other people. Stories become our principal means of getting to know other people.

2. To make a point: We often use stories to make a particular point, which becomes the moral of the story. We talk about someone going through a particular experience and learning a lesson. Sometimes we present people with problems that are similar to theirs, and our stories can reveal how someone else overcame the problem. These are known as 'isomorphic metaphors'.

3. To create states in other people: Although we might tell stories to make other people laugh, we rarely consider the art of creating powerful states with others an essential function. When you tell stories well you can create very powerful states in other people.

4. To construct yourself: Stories can also be used to construct yourself in some way. Remember, every time you describe yourself in a story and depict yourself dealing with particular situations, people are making images of you inside their heads. This helps them formulate an understanding of who you are.

The most useful attitude you can have in storytelling is to be really clear about what you want to do with the stories. For any story you tell you should be aware of the fact that you will be positioning yourself in the other person's mind in a particular way. You also need to be aware that every story is going to make the other person feel something. So if you don't ensure that you're in control of what they feel, they might well find themselves feeling bored as a result. Being a strategic storyteller is crucial to winning the hearts and minds of your audience.

You should also be aware that the stories you share don't just share experiences: they make particular points. One of the most annoying experiences you can have in a conversation is to hear someone telling a story for what seems like an eternity and then, at the very end, for them to stop and say, 'I can't remember why I'm telling you this.' Please avoid being that kind of person. Instead, always have a clear message in the stories you tell. You don't always have to articulate this at the end, but people should get the point of your story. It should add value in some way.

Thinking about stories with this kind of attitude will help you to strategically create the right kind of effect on your audience. However, to truly make a significant impact on them there are a number of skills that need to be implemented along the way.

STORYTELLING FUNDAMENTALS

Before getting into the four functions of storytelling and examining specific advice for each one, I want to focus on five core skills for telling any kind of story.

1. Your state

As I discussed earlier, the state you go into will have a strong influence on the state your audience goes into. The stories you tell them must involve you bringing them through various emotions by accessing emotions through your characters.

2. Show, don't tell

A few years ago, I did a screenwriting course. One important lesson in particular keeps coming into my mind ever since: show, don't tell. The ability to immerse someone in a story, rather than just explaining the facts of the story, is vital in ensuring that the story is memorable and full of impact.

3. The power of expression

The power you have to express yourself in your stories is absolutely vital to your ability to move people. Making people laugh and cry, inspiring them to feel motivated—these involve not only the creation of a powerful state in yourself and the acting out of a story but also *how* you act it out. Your facial expressions, timing, tone of voice—all the non-verbal and para-verbal signals you give off will add to, or detract from, the power of your stories.

Practise making a variety of faces in the mirror to convey different states in very clear ways. Practise using different voices with a wide variety of emotion. The more you can train yourself to become expressive, the easier it will be for you to shape another person's feelings when they listen to you. The reason actors are so good at affecting us is that they're excellent at expressing themselves and powerfully conveying their feelings.

4. Use subtext

Some of the best Hollywood producers and screenwriters use subtext to get messages across in a memorable way. Subtext is the undertone of an interaction, what is not said at the conversational level but is said by body language, eye contact, gesture, the context of the interaction, the past relationship between the characters and so on.

For example, when two characters are talking, what they're seemingly talking about is not always the same as what they're really talking about. A man asking a woman out for a cup of coffee could be for a simple business meeting, or it could be an indication that he is in love with her. Things are not always as they seem, and writers know that. When you tell stories, make sure to consider the conflicting messages that might be given by statements or requests, and let the audience feel that there is more than meets the eye.

5. Nesting stories

One of the factors that makes television series so popular, even addictive, is the importance of what researchers call the 'Zeigarnik effect'. This is named after the Lithuanian psychiatrist and psychologist Bluma Zeigarnik, who found that waiters were better able to remember orders before serving them than afterwards. In the same way, we're better able to remember and pay attention to stories when they're unfinished or interrupted. We've all experienced something similar when doing exams: we find ourselves remembering as much as we can right up until the end, but just a few short hours after the exam is over it's nearly impossible to remember the information we had retained for weeks leading up to it.

It seems that we have a need for closure, and when it's not provided we experience dissonance. What this means from a storytelling viewpoint is that when you tell a story it's a good idea to set up particular problems and issues requiring resolution. That way your audience will be paying closer attention in an attempt to discover how these are dealt with.

Your stories should set up challenges at the beginning and delay successfully resolving them until the last possible moment. That way it's easier to hold the attention of the audience, and when you do finally reach the resolution you will finish the story on a high.

STORY STRUCTURE

Your story should have a beginning, middle and end. Stories require conflict and the resolution of conflict to move forward. Possibly one of the best approaches to story structure comes from the notion of the 'hero's journey'.

The hero's journey

The hero's journey is one of the most popular concepts in the theory of storytelling. Joseph Campbell, in his classic work *The Power of Myth*, argues that there's a limited number of story types and that the vast majority of them involve a hero's journey. At a very basic level, here's how it can best be described:

1. *Hero is okay. All is okay.*
2. *Along comes monster. Hero fights and loses.*
3. *Hero meets guide, who teaches him how to overcome monster.*
4. *Hero faces monster again but this time defeats it with advice from guide.*
5. *Hero lives happily ever after.*

Now, I'm sure I'm going to be criticised for my simplification of this process. Nonetheless, for our purposes there are three principal elements: a hero who goes through a transformation; a source of conflict (the monster) that hurts the hero; and a lesson or experience (the guide) that teaches the hero how to overcome the conflict. The most popular films are clear examples of this, from *Star Wars* to *The Karate Kid*.

When you tell a story, often the listener will be wondering who the protagonist is. Good stories usually involve some sort of challenge or problem that is faced by the main character and that will explain how they learn to overcome it.

Many products and services these days are sold by marketing stories that follow this format. We have the former consumer of slimming bars as the hero, photos of them when they were overweight (the monster) and then of them being slim, having eaten the bars (the guide).

STORYTELLING TIPS

Finally, let's look at what you can do to help achieve each of the four functions of your stories.

Sharing experiences

Ask yourself how the story is relevant to the person or audience you're speaking to, and make sure you can emphasise the parts that are most relevant and useful to them.

Always make sure the experience you're sharing helps them learn something valuable. If necessary, connect the experience you're recounting to something very easy for them to understand and relate to.

Making points

Be very clear about exactly what your message, argument or point is and about how you would articulate it in one sentence. Find a way of getting one of the characters in your story to state the point or message clearly as part of the story. This is more powerful than you extracting that message from the story. Avoid being patronising with your stories. For example, if you're trying to convey to a smoker the message that quitting will be hard but that it will be worth it, avoid the following type of story:

> Once upon a time, there was a man who climbed a steep hill, but he thought many times he wouldn't get to the top, because he had failed so often. Eventually he decided once and for all that he would do his best, and he managed to make it to the top. It was very much worth it.

This is too obvious and can make the person feel foolish rather than positively affected. It can also irritate the listener, as it demonstrates a lack of genuine empathy on behalf of the speaker.

Creating states

Use the present tense to place the listener in the experience as effectively as possible. Avoid telling your story like this:

> Yesterday I saw something very cool. I walked down near the sea and I saw this skydiver land on a moving speedboat. I had my mouth open I was so stunned.

Instead, you could try and make the image more vivid and affecting, like this:

> Yesterday, there I was, walking near the sea, and I see this skydiver, and he's landing on this speedboat while it's still moving quickly. My jaw drops as I'm watching all this unfolding, and I'm thinking, This is stunning.

You can also switch the point of view of the story to re-create the experience more fully. For example, in this example I move from it being about me to it being something you can connect with:

> I remember my holidays when I was relaxing, because . . . You know that feeling when you're lying on the beach and you're really comfortable and really relaxed, and you've nothing to do but feel really peaceful?

Constructing yourself

Allude to the facts you want others to know while thinking about you.

> It's as if watching TV isn't always good for you. Every Monday, Tuesday and Thursday after I come home from the gym, TV's nice to relax with, all right, but you wouldn't want to be doing it too much.

This alludes to how fit you are.

Describe things in a way that enhances your own image. For example:

> I like Brian. One of the reasons is that he's so upfront and honest. I really admire that in a person. He's loyal as well. You always know where you stand with him.

This gives the impression that, because these are qualities you admire, it's likely that you possess them too.

THE 'STORYTELLING' EXERCISE

Use the first and last lines below to tell a story. Apply the various fundamentals to each story and try to achieve all four functions.

Story 1

Opening line: 'The news today reported a frog that jumped out of a tree near the train station . . .'
Final line: 'Everyone was happy in the end.'

Story 2

Opening line: 'The best and craziest holiday I ever went on was . . .'
Final line: 'Then he put his watch back in his pocket, and we never saw him again.'

Story 3

Opening line: 'The first time I saw you I thought . . .'
Final line: 'That would be horrible!'

Chapter 22

How to deliver a compelling speech

If I could just say a few words . . . I'd be a better public speaker.

HOMER SIMPSON

I'll never forget the first time I stood on stage before an audience to give a speech. I was thirteen. It was a class debate in front of about thirty people. I stood before the mocking faces, unaware that my shirt was sticking out of my trousers. I was shaking like a leaf, my hands trembling as I gripped the index cards on which my speech was written.

The cards, smeared with sweat, were so creased and torn that they became nearly impossible to read. They contained a speech my sister had written for me. The speech itself made sense, probably. But I wouldn't have known. I was far too terrified to have had a clue what I was saying. After seven minutes of blinding torture, I got to sit down, and, my face like a blood-red tomato, I curled up behind my desk, feeling the scorching heat of the smirking faces behind me.

About twenty years later, I stood in the main hall directly outside that classroom, delivering a speech to more than three hundred students, parents and teachers at a sixth-year graduation ceremony. I was extremely comfortable and enjoyed it, having been asked to be the guest of honour, the first past-pupil guest of honour at my school. The reason I was asked was because of what I now do: I travel the world and, among other things, teach people to be able to speak with confidence in public.

Now, my story is a familiar one. What frightens us most when we're young often becomes our obsession in later life. But what's interesting about my story is what happened just a few months after my very first speech. While most people might have thought that the humiliating experience was evidence that public speaking just wasn't my 'thing', I didn't feel that way. In fact, the way I felt then was that I had let myself down. The way I felt was that I couldn't actually get much lower.

You see, one of the beautiful aspects of 'dying on stage', as they call it, is that it gives you clarity. It gets you to realise, once and for all, that it doesn't matter—not nearly as much as you might think, anyway. It doesn't matter what they say, because you're going to be okay after it.

So a couple of months after this first horrific ordeal, and to the surprise of many, I signed up for the public-speaking society, for a competition against other schools, known as the 'Quantum Public Speaking' contest. This time I wrote my own speech. Interestingly, the topic of the speech was 'A Change in Thinking Can Result in a Change of Outcomes'. When I look back at it now, the irony is fascinating.

While preparing that speech, I decided to write only what I thought and felt. I decided that it would show my quirky sense of humour and my weird way of thinking—that if I was going to flop as a speaker, I was at least going to flop as myself. That evening I remember being more nervous than I had ever been before. I remember entering a room in which there were more than sixty people, most of them strangers. I remember sitting there and waiting my turn. I remember when there was just one more speaker to go before me. And I went to the bathroom.

I stood in front of the mirror and stared at myself for what seemed like an eternity. I looked deep into my own eyes and summoned up all the determination I could muster, and I gritted my teeth. Then, with no-one else around, I declared, 'This is your time. Come on, you can do it. Go for it.' With that, I marched out with steely determination, just in time for my speech. And I spoke. And they laughed. And they clapped. And I knew I had proved something important to myself.

Being a great public speaker isn't about where you stand on stage. It's not about how fancy your Powerpoint is or how clever your opening joke is. It's a mixture of how you feel about yourself, your audience and what you have to say. Most people find themselves so absorbed in what the audience is thinking that they don't get this simple truth.

THE MIND OF A GREAT SPEAKER
In fact, there's a frequently quoted survey about fears, which says that

public speaking is the greatest fear people have, even more than of death. As Jerry Seinfeld has pointed out, this means that at a funeral, people would prefer to be the one in the coffin than the one standing up giving the eulogy!

Regardless of the exact nature of such a study, it's obvious that many people suffer from a great fear of public speaking. Becoming charismatic is often sought after because it allows us to speak to a room full of people confidently and keep them engaged. In order to speak in public effectively, you have to focus on two important areas.

Firstly, you have to be in the very best possible state you can be in. You have to have the very best attitude towards standing up in front of a room full of people and establishing credibility, attention and interest. Secondly, you have to understand the keys to winning over an audience, regardless of its size. That means having a good insight into the skills that world-class speakers use to win their audiences over during their talks and speeches.

To tackle both of these areas, we will be drawing from much of what you've already learnt in this book. You learnt earlier about the importance of controlling your state and how exactly to do that; you learnt how to grab and keep people's attention when you communicate through charismatic language. Those skills are invaluable in helping you to become a great speaker. But let's go further: what are the things to keep in mind in order to be at your best with an audience?

Let's look more closely at the attitude of world-class speakers. The very best feel comfortable in front of their audience. In certain situations, they might feel adrenaline pumping, but they interpret that as excitement and as a sign that they're looking forward to giving the presentation.

The very best speakers know what they're talking about and know that they're there for one reason: to impact the audience. This is probably the biggest difference between confident and nervous speakers. Nervous speakers have their attention focused on themselves and on what the audience thinks about them. Confident speakers are focused on the audience and on what the audience needs to know, understand, feel, believe or learn. When your focus is on the audience you're absorbed in doing the best job you can rather than in trying to impress or show off. This distinction is hugely important. Whenever I work with someone to help them change the way they feel about speaking in public, this is the very first thing I want them to understand.

The second thing I want them to know is that they are the ones in control. A few years ago, in the Irish Management Institute, I worked with a woman when giving a talk on stage on presentation skills. She had a phobia about speaking in public. When I asked her what specifically frightened her most, she said, 'I hate being out of control and having all those people staring at me.' What I did was to help her understand that she was the one in control when she stepped on stage. With the woman standing beside me I said to her, 'Watch this.' I then turned to the audience and said, 'Would everyone please stand up.' They stood, some reluctantly, and then I continued, 'Would you please put your left arm out in the air and, with your right arm, touch your nose, and lift your right foot six inches off the ground. Now, please stay that way.' Once again they obeyed, at which point I turned to her and said, 'Look at how ridiculous they look. When you're the speaker they will do what you say. You're in control.'

That one insight added greatly to her confidence, and she reported that it made a big difference to how she felt on stage. When you're speaking to an audience, you control their attention, and you dictate what they are to do. Remembering that can help you to feel far more confident as a speaker.

Another important shift in attitude is to recognise the mindset of people in an audience. Most people are there to learn something. If you possess that information your main job is to convey it to them, period. Anything else you do is a bonus. Of course, if you're a professional speaker or a comedian you're expected to make them feel motivated, inspired, entertained, amused or engaged. But in reality most presentations don't require you to do any of those things.

What this means is that you have a lot less pressure on you than you might think. For example, I've experienced being the best man for my friends' weddings on three occasions. In one other instance I was asked to be groomsman and was speaking to the best man a few minutes before his speech. To calm his nerves I spelt it out for him: he was there to thank the audience, discuss the groom and talk about how beautiful the bride was. All the rest was just a bonus. The jokes didn't have to be amazing. The stories didn't have to be intriguing. His job was much simpler. After an extremely successful and popular speech, he explained that he found that change in attitude invaluable, as it really allowed him to relax and enjoy giving the speech.

The next realisation for public speaking is that people want you to succeed when you're up there. Often when you look out at an audience, they can seem ridiculously frightening, but the truth is that most people's 'concentration face' involves some form of frowning. Accepting this means you can see that, behind the frowns, there are smiles just waiting to happen. One good trick I've learnt is that when I get up in front of an audience I always imagine the audience smiling inside their mind, and my job is to make the smiles visible. Even if I don't manage it with everyone, it serves to ensure that my focus is in the right place.

Knowing what states you want to be experiencing is also important. The emotions you feel will be contagious, so the more confidently you present yourself, the more confident the audience will feel also. Critically, the more playful you are, the more playful and open your audience is likely to be as well. Also, the more passionate you feel, the more likely your audience is to feel the same way.

This means that the key is to go into the states you want your audience to be in. As I've mentioned earlier, power, playfulness, presence and passion are particularly important. The best speakers do entertain: when you think about the most charismatic presenters the world has ever seen, they all share either a powerful form of passion or a playfulness when they talk to an audience. From the villainous Adolf Hitler to the inspiring Martin Luther King, passion is an essential quality in their presentations. When you see top celebrities, television presenters and comedians, playfulness is a core ingredient in what makes them absorbing to watch. When you see spiritual gurus and shamans delivering their sermons or meetings, presence is very apparent.

Creating these states can involve using some state-management skills that we considered earlier. By using the 'charisma squared' technique (chapter 10) you can ensure that you're accessing the very best states possible, when you most need them.

SPEECH PREPARATION

Early in 2012, I was asked to be one of the speakers at a conference for call-centre managers, hosted by Sharon Ní Bheoláin, the well-known Irish newsreader and journalist. When I met Sharon, we talked for a few minutes, and what struck me was how well she knew not only the background of each speaker but also the topic itself. She was very well informed about the business issues presently facing call-centre managers, and she looked very comfortable holding the session.

It was apparent that she had prepared thoroughly and hadn't just turned up to read from a script. I also noticed that her presentation was much more full of life and personality than what she normally gets the opportunity to show when reading the news. Preparation is critical not only in writing a speech or creating slides but in actually delivering it. When you know what you're talking about, it's evident to everyone else.

It's critical to understand what you should be doing before, during and after a speech or presentation. I want to offer you a process or checklist that will come in handy for any and every presentation you will have. This process will ensure that you know how to plan, prepare and present your talk in the most effective way. In actually structuring your speech there are a few things to remember.

The 'primacy effect' is a law in psychology that states that people tend to remember what they hear first in a presentation. The 'recency effect' states that people tend to remember what they hear last in it. Because of these effects it's important that your introduction and conclusion are strong and memorable and make the point of the speech clearly and concisely.

Before any speech, here are the things to do to prepare adequately for it. There are ten core questions to ask yourself.

What do the audience believe now about you and the topic of the speech?
How will they be feeling?
What do they want from the speech?
What is important to them in a speaker and about the topic?
What do they do and how can the speech help them?
Why should they listen to you?
What do you want them to believe?
How do you want them to feel?
What do you want them to know?
What do you want them to do?

Make sure that you're in the best possible state you can be in and that you know what skills you're going to use to get them into the states you want them to be in. Be very clear about your message and make sure that you're prepared to cover all the necessary bases.

During the speech, here are the key things you need to do. It's important to walk and talk with confidence and purpose from the moment you walk onto the stage until the moment you walk off it. As you've already learnt, your body language can send signals to your brain and to the brains of others about you being a confident and credible person. Manage your energy and stay vibrant. It's essential that you learn to stay present and to be full of energy when you deliver a presentation.

Equally important is to tune in to the energy of the audience and to prepare some energy-boosters or audience-engagement techniques (see below) for when their energy drops.

Another essential factor to bear in mind is to stay on track throughout. Keep everything relevant to the presentation and to the audience, and keep answering the question 'Why should they care?' as you explain the ideas you're speaking about.

After the speech, here is a process to make automatic: collect whatever feedback you can get on how you did and find out what you can do to improve. If possible collect footage of the speech so you can go back and watch it and dissect it. Immediately afterwards mentally review the speech and ask yourself where there's room for improvement and what you did particularly well. Learning from your presentations is one of the things that marks the greatest speakers out from everyone else. Also allow yourself to bask in the warm glow of a good presentation.

SPEECH STRUCTURE
The old advice given on the structure of any speech is that in the introduction you tell them what you're going to tell them, in the body of the speech you tell them, and in the conclusion you tell them what you told them. To me, this simple strategy is a nice basic approach, but there are a few other things you need to do.

Introduction
Grab attention
The first thing you do on stage should be to immediately grab people's attention. This could be with a fascinating or hilarious story, a shocking fact or statistic, or something else you know will get the

audience thinking to themselves, 'This is going to be interesting'.

Introduce the message

The point of an introduction is really to introduce the main themes or concepts of your talk. At the beginning you should outline what you're going to talk about and explain your message concisely and clearly for the audience.

Pace the audience

It's also smart to pace the audience by setting the scene and explaining what they're already thinking. Doing so allows you to create credibility, because you seem to be reading the minds of those you're speaking to.

Keep in mind the 4-mat system

The '4-mat system' is a good one to be aware of when beginning your presentation. It suggests four steps to start any training. You answer the following questions:

> *Why learn about this?*
> *What are you going to learn?*
> *How are you going to learn and do it?*
> *How do you apply what you've learnt here in real life?*

Answer why they should listen

The question everyone has on their mind at the beginning of watching someone present a speech is 'Why should I bother listening to you?' It's a good idea to emphasise the 'why they should listen to you' part and to give them the reason at the very beginning to ensure that they're motivated to pay attention.

Speech body
State the message

Once you've introduced your subject or topic, you need to be as clear as possible when explaining your main idea or message succinctly before you go and expand on it.

Give examples

When you've stated your message clearly, make sure you then give a number of examples that explain why this idea is accurate or true.

Defend the message

It's also important to acknowledge potential counter-arguments that you might face and to explain why these aren't strong enough to disprove your idea or message.

Repeat the message

Once you've given a number of examples and taken apart the counter-arguments, you can then repeat your message so that they really get it.

Conclusion

Review the message

When you're concluding your speech, the first thing to do is to review whatever you've talked about so far. Review each message or idea you've gone through and summarise the general message.

Review the importance of the message

It's good enough just to make the point again, but you should also look to emphasise why the point is so important and to explain what it will mean for the audience. For example, begin by explaining why they should bother listening to you, and end by discussing how important your message is and how they need to take action.

Clarify the action needed

Once you explain why your message matters, next be very clear about what action they must take from your message. What do they need to do in order to follow up what you've said to them?

Conclude memorably

Lastly, you want the audience walking away from your speech feeling impacted. Think about a meaningful or memorable story that summarises the point you wanted to make. Use some of the speech devices explained below to build to a climax, when you say your final 'Thank you'. The key is to end definitely and purposefully.

Audience management

Managing the audience is about ensuring that you're in control and doing what's necessary to keep them happy and on track.

Read the audience

Pay attention to the responses of the audience. Instead of expecting everyone to look fascinated and engaged, watch their default state at the very beginning. In other words, how do they look when you begin? Any changes from that state should give you a good understanding as to what they're feeling or experiencing. And let them know. If you see them looking particularly tired you can acknowledge this and do something to help them wake up.

Connect with the audience

You can connect with the audience by explaining your message in relation to them. When preparing for the talk, you need to be very clear about what their lives or businesses are like so that they have a good idea of how what you're saying fits in with them and their life.

Also, continually observe how they're experiencing the talk and let them know you understand what they're feeling or thinking.

Establish credibility

Building credibility with the audience is about ensuring that you position yourself with the seven pillars of persuasion so that you come across as confident, expert, likeable, similar to them, engaging, trustworthy and open.

Stimulate the audience

Regularly during the speech or workshop you should be looking for ways to get them really engaged with what you're talking about. Most talks follow a format of peaks and troughs, in that there will be periods of high and low engagement. If you can minimise the periods of low engagement and make sure that every dip is followed by a point of high engagement you will be in a much better position. You can use a number of speech devices (see below) that can stimulate the audience and create a high point of engagement.

AUDIENCE ENGAGEMENT

Impacting the audience and engaging them involves using a number of speech devices to grab their attention and to make your ideas and messages more memorable. It's also about getting them in the right kind of states to take in information effectively. Here are twelve devices you can use.

1. Repetition

If you really want someone to remember an idea and take it in, it's essential that you repeat it. This book, for example, repeats many concepts over and over again. It does so because these concepts are so important: it's absolutely critical that you get them and that they become the foundation for new action. Frank Luntz, an American political consultant, explains it best.

> There's a simple rule: You say it again, and you say it again, and you say it again, and you say it again, and you say it again, and then again and again and again and again, and about the time that you're absolutely sick of saying it is about the time that your target audience has heard it for the first time.

2. Contrasts

The writer and graphic designer Nancy Duarte explained at a fascinating TEDX conference how to use contrast to make your speech better. Contrasts are often used effectively by speakers to draw attention to the differences between their argument and the opposing one. The idea is that, by polarising the two concepts, they make their concept all the more compelling. There's also a powerful rhythm to this technique. For example John F. Kennedy's 'Ask not what your country can do for you. Ask what you can do for your country.'

3. Rule of three

For some reason, whenever we hear someone giving us a list of items it only feels like the list is complete after we hear the third item. Our brains are used to hearing things in threes, so speakers will often incorporate threes in their presentations in order to produce a greater effect. Here are two examples in the classic speech by Abraham Lincoln known as the Gettysburg Address: 'We can not dedicate—we can not consecrate—we can not hallow—this ground.' 'Government of the people, by the people, for the people.'

4. Rhetorical questions

Rhetorical questions are in the form of questions but are not asked with the expectation of a reply, as they imply the answer themselves. They can be used very powerfully in making a particular point memorable. People tend to remember messages when they're in the form of an implied response. 'Can you see how much impact this can have?' 'Do you realise why this works so well?'

5. Jokes

Using humour is another highly effective tool for shaping an audience's emotional state, enabling them to remember information more effectively, as well as positioning yourself as someone fun to listen to. In the chapter on making people laugh (chapter 20) you will have learnt various ways to do this.

6. Quotations

Using quotations is a very successful way of getting a message across to an audience. When you quote someone two things happen. Firstly, the audience don't see the message as coming directly from you. Therefore it doesn't seem like you're trying to convince them of it (so they tend to take it in more easily). Secondly, you can use the credibility of whoever you quote in order to make your message more compelling. (It's not just you who believes your message but also person x.) As Brian Colbert once explained, 'quotations are a really effective way of getting your message across.'

7. Stories

Telling a good story is a brilliant way of impacting the audience. Often presidential candidates will tell their audience a story about a particular person they met who was experiencing something that many in their audience have been going through. They will show how they helped that person and listened to them, so you feel that the person they're talking about represents you and that the problem or issue they have is representative of yours. They will also tell stories to inspire you and motivate you and to make you feel connected to them. You can find all you need for telling a story in the most powerful way in chapter 21.

8. Metaphors

Metaphors are a very effective way of engaging the emotions of an audience. It's no coincidence that they're used so often in the vast majority of the greatest speeches. Metaphors allow us to understand a concept in far more vivid terms. For more on metaphors see chapter 18, on charismatic language.

9. Examples

Giving an example of something is also a good way of making an impact with what you're saying. The key is to give an example of how you would use the idea, principle or skill in a number of different contexts relevant to the audience. So, for example, if you were talking about having a more positive attitude you might give an example of what a positive attitude would be in dealing with failing an exam (or something relevant to the audience you're speaking to).

10. Statistics

Statistics can also be quite useful in making a powerful impression on an audience. When you can present a statistic that's clear, surprising and important you will make them feel like your message has strong evidence to back it up, and they're more likely to believe what you're saying.

11. Rhythm and tone

The tone of voice you use and the rhythm with which you speak have a powerful effect on the audience. It's essential to understand how this rhythm works, as it can enable you to keep the audience moving between the different states you want them in.

If you get a chance to listen to the very best speakers, like Martin Luther King, Bill Clinton or JFK, you will hear them all use rhythm in powerful ways. Even if you don't understand the strategic power of their language, you can still feel yourself being affected by the musical quality of the way they present it.

12. Using slides and visual tools

Especially when making business presentations, the use of slides and visual tools is quite important. Not only does it help the audience to learn and remember information visually in a more effective way but it also positions you as an up-to-date and modern speaker and trainer.

THE 'SPEECH DEVICES' EXERCISE

All these speech devices can help you to make a positive difference with your speeches. So for each device write down a two-page snippet of a presentation you have to give, and try to use at least three examples of the twelve devices in the script. The more you practise them deliberately like this, the more likely you are to use them automatically when you present it.

Another good idea is to consult some of the most famous speeches and analyse the use of the twelve speech devices in them.

———

Now that we've had a chance to explore four essential skills for the charismatic communicator, it only remains for us to take a look at the various contexts in which these attitudes, actions and abilities will come in handy. In the next section you'll learn how to apply the charismatic edge to a number of areas of your life and business. Prepare to be spoon-fed!

Part 4

Stand for: The applications of charisma

In theory, there is no difference between theory and practice. In practice, there is.

YOGI BERRA

As I mentioned earlier, a book came out in 2006 that took the world of self-help and personal development by storm. It was called *The Secret*, but it wasn't much of a secret, as millions of people around the world bought it. It was based on a film by an Australian television-writer and producer, Rhonda Byrne, in which various popular self-help gurus discuss the law of attraction. This law suggests that you will attract into your life whatever you focus your attention on.

Now, this idea is extremely appealing. The notion that you can just think about something and make it happen is something that took the collective imagination of the positive-thinking movement by storm and excited them in its possibilities. The reality, though, is that the secret doesn't work on its own: it's only one part of the jigsaw.

Yes, I'm very sure that if you think the right kind of thoughts it's going to help you. But it's not just about doing that. The core of both the book you now hold in your hands and *The Secret* is that they promise a better future. 'Think about what you want and you'll have it,' suggests *The Secret*. 'Change your attitude and actions, learn new abilities, and you can have a better future,' I suggest here. But I'm going to add something that's needed in both cases in order to get results: you must actually follow through. It's pointless understanding the new attitude unless it's going to be part of how you think from now on. There's no point in reading and learning the actions unless you're going to carry them out. All the abilities and skills in the world are devoid of value unless you actually learn to master them. Therefore the key to making all this work is in one word: application.

In this section, I want to explore how you can use what you've learnt so far in a number of different contexts in personal and professional life. So far you've learnt many useful skills for creating the kind of impressions you want in the minds of other people. What I want to investigate now, though, is how specifically you can apply these skills in the real world—in your world—in the areas you most want to work on.

You've bought this book for a reason. Maybe it's to help you in your professional life to be a more effective leader or businessperson. Maybe you've invested in this book to develop your personal life so you can have more of a social life, improve your relationships or win over the person of your dreams.

Whatever the reason, you have a goal, and it can be achieved by communicating more effectively. If you stop reading at this stage you would find that you already have exactly what you need in order to get the results you want. But I want to make it even easier for you. I want to walk you through how to take what you've learnt and make it count.

The advice that follows will emphasise certain things over and over again, but all of it will be carefully tailored to various specific issues. Based on what you've already learnt, I'm going to walk you through, step by step, the most useful attitudes, actions and abilities for you to use in a variety of situations.

You're going to find that the following section breaks many of the actions and abilities into specific tasks to practise. This is to ensure that there's a clear set of guidelines for you to follow.

Whether you want to be more charismatic in your social life, your relationships or your life as a parent, whether you want to be a better flirt and attract others more easily or make a speech on a special occasion, this section will provide you with lots of specific suggestions as to how to do all this in the best possible way.

If the business side of things is of more interest to you, you'll learn how to master the art of the business interview and business presentation and how to become a better networker or salesperson. You'll understand how to be a more charismatic leader and how to present yourself in the best possible way in these contexts.

This section is all about how you can take charge of these situations and understand how to get the edge in them all. Through the 3D-charisma framework you'll get a special insight into exactly how to put into practice all of what you've learnt so far.

Personal-life applications

Chapter 23
Social life

Nine-tenths of the people were created so you would want to be with the other tenth.

HORACE WALPOLE

In January 2011, as part of research for a book I was working on, I was travelling in Central America, and I met an Italian guy called Tomas while hiking up a volcano near Antigua in Guatemala. Tomas and I ended up travelling for the next few weeks together, as we were going in the same direction. The next few weeks provided lots of entertainment as we made our way through El Salvador, Honduras and Nicaragua, towards Costa Rica. In Nicaragua, we even visited the hospital together after we crashed our motorbike head-on into a wall at fifty miles an hour. I say 'we'. I was actually driving, and he was on the back. But it was the bike that had the problem. I swear.

Anyway, Tomas was built like a tank and was full of charm. He was very flirtatious and got a lot of female attention because of his six-pack abs and physique. I nicknamed him Spartacus. What was really interesting to me over those few weeks was that Spartacus and I were very different in personality. His interests were different from mine in almost everything except travel. Yet we bonded as kindred spirits. Here's my point: he had the same quality that all the people that I count as my friends have. He was real. He was himself.

You see, I really do have the most amazing set of friends in the world. I'm pretty super at spotting people I resonate with and at connecting with them. They might be all different in personality—they're from a wide selection of countries and are a very diverse bunch of characters—but they all appeal to certain parts of me. But it's not really by accident or even because I'm such a great person to be friends with. In reality, it's something I make an effort at. It's not really a big effort, but it's an effort nonetheless.

In the modern world, with everyone having a plethora of Facebook friends, it would seem that most people have a wild social life. The reality is that that's quite far from the truth. Indeed, now more than ever, people need to find ways of building on and improving their social life in person. As social media has changed the game, relationships have become more superficial.

So, in this world of surface-level connections, how do you build a better social life? The word 'loneliness' is still an extremely common search term, with more than 40 million results on Google. Many people crave company and someone to relate to. In order to be in the best possible position to build a better social life, here are some suggestions on what to think, do and practise.

ATTITUDE

Here are some thoughts to dwell on.

In order to be liked, you must be likeable. In order to be likeable, you must like yourself and hence be nice to yourself. The truth is that if you hate yourself and would find it painful to hang around with yourself, how can you expect anyone else to find it any different? So, be nice.

Most people are friendly—it just takes more time and effort for some. Deep down, behind every nasty facial expression there's a beaming smile waiting to be discovered. Even if it isn't there, this attitude will make it far more likely that you will find it.

Everyone is a potential friend, but some people are better for you than others. Be open to the right kind of friends, though only to those who add value and good feelings to your life. If they suck the self-confidence and cheery mood out of you, let them be friends with someone else.

Being yourself is the most important thing you can do. This is my key message. Lots of people spend too much time trying to be someone else so they can have what someone else has. Then they realise they can't be that person, so they look to be some other person. Being yourself is far easier and will make you a lot happier.

Along the way, of course, friends are going to make mistakes. So are you. You need to learn to get over it—unless it's too many mistakes that make too big an impact and happen too often. Give your friends a break and yourself a break . . . for a while. But never accept disrespect and bad treatment from them if it becomes a regular occurrence. There are plenty of friend-fish in the sea! You don't need anyone bad for you in your life. Treat them the way they deserve to be treated, and if you notice that you aren't doing it, start now.

Rejection is about the other person: it's a reflection of their mistaken perception. If they don't want to hang around with you it's their loss. Feel sorry for them. They got it wrong. Focus on the ones who made the smart move. If you feel that you have no friends, remember that even the biggest bastards in history have had friends, so it's not a measure of worth. You can find friends if you meet enough people. The key is to find really good friends. That requires you to be a really good friend.

ACTIONS
Once your attitude is in check, the next step is to do the kind of things that are necessary in building friends and a social group.

Make the other person feel important
Everyone loves to feel important. The best way to show an interest in someone is to be genuinely interested in them and their life. Ask yourself what's interesting about the other person. You will always find something if you look hard enough.

Look after how you look and sound, and your sense of style
Practise looking charismatic, speaking charismatically and dressing and grooming to accentuate your assets and reduce your weaknesses.

Watch your gestures
Pay attention to your smile and hand movements, to the way you eat and drink and to your walk and facial expressions. Try to come across as open and approachable.

Practise smiling
This is absolutely essential in socialising. People don't want to hang around with a sourpuss. Practise smiling different kinds of smile in the mirror. While some will entice, others will frighten. Become more aware of when you are and aren't smiling. And enjoy it—nothing worse than a faker!

Shaking hands

Again, this is basic, but some people still crush hands, and some give you the goldfish handshake, where it's weak and limp. The key is to be firm—but not too firm—and to accompany the handshake with a smile. Imagine passing good feelings through your hands to them and try and do it. It can feel like that to them!

Touching

The power of touch has been shown in many cases to foster better relationships between people. Try and ensure when talking to others that you touch them briefly in some way.

Stay in contact

Once you meet a person for the first time and get their details, follow it up the next day with an email or text. Then, a few days later, send them a link to something connected with what you spoke about. This is extremely powerful, as it puts the relationship in a new context, with possibilities for the future.

Create rapport

Practise matching body language, gestures and use of language. By mirroring what you see, the other person will feel closer to you after the interaction.

Read them better

If you want to truly connect with someone it's important that you get to know them as well as you can. Often, if you pay enough attention to them when you meet them for the first time you can get a good understanding of whether or not they're long-term friend material.

Abilities
Name recall

When you're being introduced to someone, repeat their name as you look at them and repeat it inside your head several times. The key is to listen to them when they say their name instead of being busy focusing on something else in the interaction. People get annoyed at you when you don't remember who they are—and they like you more when you do.

Listen

Listen to what people actually say. Listen to the words they like to use and their expressions. The more you hear these, the better you'll be at responding to them in a way that they understand and appreciate. Being a good listener is about being able to understand where the other person is coming from and then demonstrating that—not to become a dead wall. Listening is not about shutting up: it's about actually taking in what they're explaining to you.

Praise

The secret to a good compliment is to praise the person for something unique that you actually do like and then to follow it with a short justification. When you're just being honest and you seem not to have any ulterior motives, people tend to feel that you're speaking truthfully.

Demonstrate politeness

Wherever you go, treat everyone with the same level of respect, whether they're a top businessman or a waiter. When you do so in front of others you will gain credibility and respect yourself. Be polite and courteous. Always say hello and thank you, and smile at those who serve you.

Become funnier and a better storyteller

It's useful to demonstrate reasons why people would like to be around you. Making people laugh and engaging them in your stories are two effective ways to do this.

Chapter 24
Flirting

There are times not to flirt. When you're sick. When you're with children. When you're on the witness stand.

JOYCE JILLSON

Before I even start on this chapter, I can hear the cynics with their voices dipped in sarcasm. 'Oh, look, Mr Charisma is going to teach us how to flirt. Go on, then, Mr Sex God, tell us how to become more attractive.' Now, the reality is that I'm no seduction teacher. It's not my 'thing'. The idea of memorising lines and 'peacocking' just doesn't appeal to me when I go out. ('Peacocking' is a term used by seduction teachers to describe the fact that if you dress a bit differently and stand out it shows confidence and offers a potential topic of conversation.) For me, it's about being yourself. But not just any version of yourself: the best version of yourself.

There's an entire industry dedicated to teaching people (especially men) attraction or flirting skills. My friend and colleague Leopi, author of *The Leopi Effect*, is one of the better teachers in the area of attraction, and much of what he teaches is in alignment with the ideas in this book.

So, what is the art of flirting? It's about playfully conversing with another person in a way that fosters attraction and enjoyment. In a perfect world there would be no need for games when two people meet. However, when two people do meet, games are quite often used for this purpose

The following advice is not necessarily useful, and it can in some ways be detrimental to a relationship once it's under way. Relationships are formed on the basis of the initial phase of attraction and of 'falling for' the other person. The ideas given below definitely help to foster and promote this. However, actually having a good relationship is a completely different story that relies on the two people being good to each other and being honest and caring in every way. Instead of holding feelings back they should be expressed in the best way. Do remember this when you find the right person—or if you already have.

You aren't guaranteed to meet the right person for you after following these suggestions, but it will certainly help you not to mess it up when you do. Oh, and, obviously, try not to make the mistake I made with the attempted smile I told you about earlier!

ATTITUDE

Your attitude is crucial when it comes to flirting or attraction. If you want to get who you want, you need to let go of neediness. Show someone that you really want them but that you don't really need them. Remember, there's nothing so unattractive as someone who is needy. So, begin to concentrate more on other areas of your life and focus on how happy you are with what you already have.

People most want what they must work to have. In the early stages avoid leaving a person certain of your affections. When you're speaking with them let them take over your world. Then, every once in a while, pull back and act uninterested or distant. The more uncertain they are of you, the more they'll be focused on trying to win you over, instead of on evaluating you. Of course, it's important to stay respectful and avoid treating the other person badly while doing this.

It's also smart to act towards people as if they could become your new best friend. With this belief in your head you will be more likely to act in a way that makes people like you and feel friendly towards you.

Settle only for the best for you. Avoid being with someone just to be in a relationship. At the same time, it's not clever to go only for ridiculously gorgeous models just because it serves your ego. Let yourself be prepared to be happy alone but open to opportunities to connect and you'll be amazed at what the universe will do for you.

There's no such thing as *the* right person: there's only *a* right person—and they're not perfect. There are a few people who would be 'right' for you. By this I mean they're simply people with whom you have great chemistry and that you know you're compatible with. Avoid searching for 'the one' and instead be open to a wonderful person coming into your life.

Confidence is gorgeous. Laughter is beautiful. Fun is addictive.

The more confident you appear, the more attractive you will appear. The more you make someone laugh, the more attractive you will be to them. The more fun they have with you—yep, you guessed it: the more attractive you will be.

ACTIONS
So, what are the key behaviours or actions of charismatic flirts?

Make the other person feel important
Everyone loves to feel important. The best way to show an interest in someone is to be genuinely interested in them and their life.

Stay outside your head
Instead of mumbling all that stuff in your head about what a person is thinking, repeat the mantra 'Shut up now, shut up now, shut up now.' When you do this, after a while your brain learns to stop giving you such a hard time and will let you just relax and be in the moment, focusing on the positives.

Be aware of how you look and sound and of your sense of style
Practise looking charismatic, speaking charismatically and dressing and grooming to accentuate your assets and reduce your weaknesses.

Watch your gestures
Pay attention to your smile, your hand movements, the way you eat and drink, your walk and the expressions you use. A good way to find out about these is to ask one of your best friends to impersonate you in each of these. This will reveal to you how other people see you and will give you valuable insights into what you need to do to stop or start coming across in a certain way.

Look after yourself
Get fit, tone your body, eat and sleep well. Healthy is sexy.

Walk charismatically
The 'Alexander technique', developed by the actor Frederick Matthias Alexander, offers a useful way of improving your posture and walk. Try relaxing the muscles in the neck and shoulders. By doing so you'll find your body instantly feeling more relaxed and 'lifted'. Next, if you

imagine a puppet string lifting your head you'll find yourself walking straight and tall in a natural way, which will create the impression of confidence and composure.

Practise smiling

Practise smiling at people and holding their gaze a couple of seconds longer than would be considered normal. Also practise smiling different kinds of smile in the mirror. While some will entice, others will frighten!

Be mysterious

Never talk too much about yourself. The more a person doesn't know about you, the more they'll feel they want to know.

Get out there, gorgeous

Stop making excuses and lazing about. If it's really important to you to find that 'right' person, make yourself available and get out there! Meet as many people as possible and make sure you're always dressed to kill. Join clubs and societies and put yourself in a situation where you meet people with similar interests.

Play scarce

Never spend too much time with the person to whom you're attracted. Talk to them for a while and then, when they're most enjoying the conversation, make an excuse to leave for a while. Be aware and in control of the dynamic of the conversation, and always leave them wanting more.

ABILITIES

Lastly, what are the specific skills that are important in being at your best when wooing a potential partner?

Remember names

Remembering a person's name helps you get on better with them, which, in turn, helps you have more of a chance with them.

Become funnier

Have more of a laugh with those you talk to when you're out. Playfully joke around, tease others, make light-hearted fun of yourself, be cocky and funny and develop your humour skills.

Take bold action when you feel an opportunity arises
When you see an opportunity to move forward and ask for a date or to kiss someone, go for it immediately. When you take bold action, it demonstrates absolute confidence. Anything else and you risk losing the chance.

Get the other person focused on trying to impress you, not on analysing if you're 'good enough'
The more someone is trying to impress you, the less they're evaluating you. Hence they're presupposing that you're good enough for them. The way to make them do this is by teasing them a bit playfully and demonstrating that you're still evaluating them to see if they're good enough. Mixing this with obvious signs of attraction keeps them on their toes.

Tell them stories
If you want to get to know the other person, listen to their stories. If you want them to get to know you, tell them your stories. People don't fall for your opinions or for facts about you: they fall for the way you tell your story. Stories can capture their imagination, lead them into your life by the hand and show them around your life.

Focus on them, not on you
Remember, it's much less important how you come across than it is how you make the other person feel. Even just saying hello and being yourself, without any clever jokes or lines, can work wonders—as long as the emphasis is on how to make the other person feel good and not on how they will evaluate you.

Make them feel like a hero or princess
Even in this age of political correctness, most women still love to be treated like princesses, and men still love to be treated like heroes. In same-sex relationships, there's also often a desire for strong male and female qualities. Be chivalrous or ladylike and allow the other person to see your masculinity or femininity. By letting them see that side of you, you make it clear that there's a sexual side to you. In this way you make it more likely for them to see you in a sexual way. It's all about yin and yang.

Practise one-way compliments

Practise giving honest, sincere compliments to people you haven't met and then walking away. Avoid expecting anything back from them. This gets you into the habit of doing it for the right reason: to make them feel good, not to make you look good. Imagine it's your job to make them feel wonderful about themselves.

Key-word awareness

Listen for the other person's key words. There will be words they like and use a lot. Use these occasionally to make them feel like you think as they do.

Demonstrate abundance

Create the impression in the other person that money is not your highest value. It lets them know that you're not reliant on external things, and it creates around you an aura of independence and strength.

Chapter 25
Relationships

Some people ask the secret of our long marriage. We take time to go to a restaurant two times a week. A little candlelight, dinner, soft music and dancing. She goes Tuesdays, I go Fridays.

HENNY YOUNGMAN

Since your partner is likely to know you pretty well, it would seem that becoming more 'charismatic' a partner would hardly be necessary. However, with separation and divorce rates as high as ever, your ability to make a positive impact on the love of your life is extremely important.

Now, I'm not exactly what you'd call a top-notch expert on relationships, as I've not had enough experience of having been in one for very long. (Honestly, it's not me, it's them!) So, as my options disappear, I think I'm going to 'phone a friend' on this one and reach for what the research says, as well as for what I've learnt from my good friends who are in happy long-term relationships.

John Gottman is regarded as one of the world's foremost experts on relationships. He conducted a fascinating longitudinal study on long-term relationships and found a highly successful strategy, with an accuracy of 91 per cent, for predicting divorce or break-ups, according to how a couple communicated with each other. The study monitored conversations between couples over a number of weeks, and after examining how they communicated with each other Gottman discovered patterns in what occurred. This enlightening research pointed to a number of critical factors in how couples argue, rather than in how often they argue. So, I want teach you how to argue. Er, no . . . Actually, there's more to it than that!

Gottman suggests that it's not unhealthy for couples to fight, but it is unhealthy for them to fight in a particular way. He describes negative behaviours and suggests alternatives for massively improving the closeness of your relationship. These alternatives are explored in depth in his book *The Seven Principles for Making Marriage Work*.

In this chapter, I've combined Gottman's suggestions with plenty of other core advice for building a better relationship with your partner. Don't ask me if it works. But it sounds pretty good to me.

ATTITUDE

Here are some of the most important beliefs to remember when you're in a relationship.

Firstly, you deserve to be treated really well by your partner, and they deserve the same. Remembering this, instead of trying to keep score, tends to help you keep your eye on what's important. You have different emotional needs from those of your partner, and you should know them both. Not only are men from Mars and women from Venus, but some men and women seem like they're from Pluto. You need to understand each other as much as possible so you can get on better. This works the exact same way in same-sex couples. You need to tune in to your partner rather than make assumptions that they're either just like you or radically different from you.

There will always be ups and downs. That's okay, and it can make you stronger. Some people get lost in the idea that relationships should be as perfect as those on television—relationships where they gaze at each other and tell each other how amazing they are. That's vomit-inducing. Ups and downs work because we need variety in our relationships. We need to be challenged and we need to learn to adapt and grow. Conflict can help us do this. The key is to ensure that the downs are not destructive to either person's sense of self.

If they reject you, it's not about them rejecting you: it's usually about them. Most of the time, when people reject you it's the result of their neurochemistry. They no longer feel what they felt, because their brain isn't mixing the same chemicals. It's not about you suddenly becoming undesirable.

Relationships should be continually worked on and never taken for granted. The worst thing you can do is to assume that since you're married or live together it's all done. Your job is to support them, love them and care for them, and theirs for you. It requires effort, but it's worth it in the long run.

You got together for a reason and it was probably a good one. It's a good idea to reflect on what you saw in them in the beginning and see if those qualities are still there. Sometimes we forget and we just need to remember.

When you're happier without them than with them in the long term, it's time to move on. There may come a time when you're better off going your separate ways. You need to be honest and accept this if the time comes. This means avoiding the comfort-zone issue that arises when you feel that it's easy to stay in a relationship even if you know it's not the right thing.

ACTIONS

Here are some great suggestions for what you can do to improve your relationship:

Arguments

- If you've got an issue to bring up, do it nicely. Research shows that arguments that begin harshly are far more dangerous to your relationship than others.
- If you have a complaint, focus on the problematic behaviour and what new behaviour you'd like to see instead.
- Avoid criticising the person themselves in a general or long-term way. For example, say 'I didn't like it when you did that; could you do something else in future?' rather than 'You're always doing that; you're so mean.'
- If you're attacked, avoid being defensive. Instead, focus on the solution to the issue or problem.
- Express how you feel once you're in a calm enough state to do that. Expressing how you feel when the emotional part of your brain (the amygdala) has taken over is never a good idea.
- Keep an eye on your body language and avoid giving negative signs of contempt or disgust to your partner. Keep your body language open as much as you can.
- Always search for a compromise and remember that your relationship is far more important than almost any other single issue.

Getting closer

- Still dress up and look good for your partner. It makes them feel valued.
- Make time for friends and keep your own independence as well. Two individuals in a relationship can get much closer than two

people who base their entire lives around the other person.
- Occasionally surprise your partner with a nice present.
- Play games with each other and get to know each other as much as possible.
- Practise remembering the best times you've had and reinterpret any challenges in a way that makes them look better.
- Go out on dates and organise things to look forward to.
- Find shared interests and activities that you can do together.
- Talk regularly about what's going on in your world.
- Focus on making your partner feel really good when they're around you.
- Pay attention to your partner's body language and non-verbal cues so that you know how they're feeling.
- Compliment your partner and make them feel regularly cherished, loved and cared for.

If children come along
- Children coming along will affect your relationship. The key is to keep remembering that you're still a partner, as well as a mother or father.
- When the children are old enough to have a babysitter, arrange a date night once a week with your partner on which you spend a romantic evening together.
- Show affection to each other in front of your children. Not too much, but the right amount will help them get a good model for a happy and contented relationship. Likewise, avoid nasty behaviour, as that can have a detrimental effect.

ABILITIES
Become funnier
Laughter is really important in long-term relationships. Seriousness is a big 'buzz kill'.

Master the skill of making them feel good
Whenever you want to convince your partner of something, the key is to focus on the emotional side of persuasion and on how to maximise how good you make them feel. The techniques and skills you learnt in part 3 will help you do that more effectively.

Tell your story even better

I believe that people fall in love with the way you tell your story. Make sure your stories remind your partner of how great you both are together and of how you're such a great team. You both need to live in your story more. Build a narrative with each other and learn to tell it in a way that re-creates the best kind of feelings associated with it.

Seduction

Often people think of seduction as being a skill to use only when you meet someone for the first time. It could be argued that it's far more useful and appropriate to use it to seduce your long-term partner. By setting a romantic scene and paying attention to getting all the details right to create the perfect atmosphere, you're more likely to make your partner feel excited about some quality intimate time together.

Relationship skills

Building a wonderful relationship means continually learning more about your partner and yourself, and working at getting closer. It means paying attention to what's going on and handling conflict by using the skills you've learnt.

Chapter 26
Parenting

Every word, facial expression, gesture, or action on the part of a parent gives the child some message about self-worth. It is sad that so many parents don't realise what messages they are sending.

VIRGINIA SATIR

One of the things I get approached about a lot on my charisma courses is suggestions for how the skills people have learnt in the course can help their children develop confidence and charisma. The question that arises is 'How do I help my child grow up to feel good about themselves and become an effective communicator so that they have a better future?'

Since my theory asserts that babies are naturally charismatic, to me the key is to help children unlearn the limiting fears that hold them back and to make sure they feel comfortable in fully being themselves as much as possible. They need to learn that they're wonderful just the way they are and that any necessary changes are merely behavioural changes and not personality changes.

In this chapter, I'd like to offer some ideas on how to think about children and charisma in relation to how you can start to do the right things to help your children improve the way they feel about themselves. I'll also explain how you can use some of the skills you've been learning to have an even more positive impact on your children's lives.

ATTITUDE
Children learn by example, not just by what you tell them. You have to show them how to treat themselves by treating yourself in the exact same way. If you berate yourself they will learn to berate themselves . . . even if you keep being positive to them.

Children are born with natural charisma. It's great to realise that children are naturally charismatic. From birth they're confident and sure of themselves. So, it's about doing what you can to help them carry these feelings through the various stages of their development.

The fears of failure, rejection and embarrassment can stifle them, so it's important to demonstrate that these three experiences aren't so bad. The more children are afraid of failing or of embarrassing themselves, the less likely they are to show their authentic and true selves to others, and the more likely they are to restrict their personalities. It's crucial that you create the kind of environment in which all three experiences are looked at in a constructive way. By constructive I mean that you make sure that you're supporting them regardless of what happens.

Encourage your children to be as animated as possible. The more animated you are when you tell them a story, for example, the more animated they will learn to be. Put on the characters' voices and make sure you animate your communication and get them used to being stimulated every time you talk to them. They will feel not only more stimulated but will also become more stimulating themselves.

Challenges must be embraced in front of the children so that they learn to do the same. Whenever you face a challenge, what matters to your children is how you handle that challenge. Make sure that, whatever happens, you deal with it in front of them by displaying qualities of leadership and confidence, of being composed and relaxed. In doing so you will teach them to become better leaders and will get them to realise that, no matter what happens, everything is going to be okay.

ACTIONS
Here are some key behaviours to practise with your children:

- Whenever they get **rejected**, explain that it's the result of a **lack of information** on the part of the other person or of the specific context. Obviously do this in a normal-sounding way! **Reaffirm their value** as a person.
- Whenever you get rejected, explain that it's the result of a lack of information on the part of the other person or of the specific context. **Reaffirm your value** out loud as a person.
- Whenever your child doesn't succeed ask them the question, **'What could you do differently next time?'**

- Whenever you don't succeed ask yourself out loud the question, **'What could I do differently next time?'**
- Place an emphasis on taking some time to **play with your children** and on **acting silly**. Let them see that acting silly is often okay and that it can help you to have fun.
- **Let your children know how special and unique they are** and that they can do things nobody else can.
- **Spend time watching the most charismatic people on television and play games** with your children in which you all imitate these characters—anyone from charismatic television hosts to comedians, from presidents to famous musicians.

ABILITIES

Here are some important skills to practise and master to help your children become more charismatic:

- **Master the art of telling stories** that affect your child's state and that help them learn lessons. Children respond particularly well to stories.
- When telling stories **practise being very animated**. The more animated you are, the more personality you put into the story and the more the child learns to be animated themselves when they tell stories.
- **Use humour** as much as possible and teach your children to have a great sense of humour about problems they might face.
- **Speak in public** in front of them and encourage them to speak in public whenever possible, helping them see that it's no big deal.
- Guide them towards the kind of behaviours that will help them grow by **connecting what you want with what they want** and by persuading them to perceive the link.

Chapter 27
Speeches for special occasions

Make sure you have finished speaking before your audience has finished listening.

DOROTHY SARNOFF

I've been lucky enough to have delivered three best-man speeches and a number of keynote and after-dinner talks. I've found that there seems to be a best practice in doing this kind of event. Usually you're expected to speak in a light and relaxed way and to make a few important points about the purpose of the evening or about the people who are there.

When I refer to giving speeches for special occasions, I'm not necessarily referring to business events. These speeches (best man-speeches, toasts and so on) are often given by people who are not used to speaking in public, so a few tips on applying the charismatic lessons of this book to this kind of situation might come in handy.

The art of making a speech for a special occasion is about understanding what you're there for and what's expected of you. With this in mind, what are the most useful attitudes, actions and abilities to have?

ATTITUDE
Your audience often doesn't expect much. As you're not a professional speaker your audience isn't expecting you to be hilariously funny or entertaining. This means there's no pressure on you to perform perfectly. You've been asked to talk, so the fact of you talking is

valuable in and of itself. Often when you're asked to speak on special occasions it's because of who you are and not because of what you say. So, anything you say that's informative or entertaining is a bonus.

You are in control. Remember, you are in control of the audience. You can make them stand, sit or touch their toes, and you can make them smile—all by telling them to do so.

If there are any silences or 'embarrassing moments', remember that nothing is embarrassing unless you make it so. What's vital to understand is that embarrassment is something that can be avoided by thinking in a particular way. It's possible to make every experience comfortable. You can also use certain prepared 'saves', such as saying, 'Well, that didn't go the way it was supposed to,' when something goes wrong, which will make the audience laugh and help release the tension.

The state the audience feels itself in is up to you. You can get your audience in the right emotional state and frame of mind by going into that state yourself. Also, it's easier to get groups to feel powerful emotions, because the emotions of the people around you tend to make you feel the same way. So, get them laughing and you'll find that they'll laugh as a group.

They won't always reflect what they feel. Remember, even when your audience look serious or are frowning they will often be smiling inside. In groups people rarely look how they feel. They get trapped in a group mask in which they don't want to stand out, so they keep still as much as possible.

The key with many special-occasion speeches is that you know at least some of the audience. Having friendly faces in the crowd makes any speech easier, as you know that they're willing you on to succeed.

ACTIONS

As well as having a better attitude about doing speeches for special occasions, it's a good idea to understand what you can do to make your speech go really well.

- Dress appropriately for the occasion.
- Practise delivering the speech many times before the event. Time yourself each time.
- Stand with one foot in front of the other and avoid locking your knees. This ensures that you have solid balance and that you can turn and have depth in front of an audience.

- Breathe comfortably and effectively when you're on stage.
- Make everything more animated. Use hand gestures and facial expressions a little bit more than normal, but do so naturally.
- As soon as you get on stage, smile and look as many of the audience members in the eye as you can. When you say hi or hello and introduce yourself, say it with as much personal warmth as possible.
- Thank all the relevant people. Most special-occasion speeches involve a lot of thank-yous. If you do this you make the special people feel special.
- Practise the presentation skills noted in part 3.

ABILITIES
Preparation
Whenever you're preparing a special speech, keep the following questions in mind:

What do I want to accomplish with this presentation?

Who do I need to thank or acknowledge?

What do I need to say or include in my speech?

Who are my audience?

What do my audience want to hear?

What do they want to feel?

What stories can I use to entertain them while making my points?

What context am I presenting in and what are the appropriate rules?

Who comes before and after me?

How do I want to start?

How do I want to finish?

Delivery
Start memorably

Start with a joke or quotation or powerful story to grab the audience's attention from the very beginning. This will create a great frame for the speech and will get them listening immediately. It's obviously also important to ensure that it relates to the theme of the speech.

Introduce yourself and do the thank-yous

Introduce yourself at the start and explain what you're doing there. This is also an opportunity to thank the various people you need to thank.

Use stories

Stories are great ways of keeping the audience engaged and interested. Think through different stories that create the kind of emotions you want in your audience.

Use quotations

When you quote someone, it enables you to put across a point in a powerful and succinct way and lends authority to your viewpoints.

Use humour

Master the art of using comedy in your speeches. It's not just about telling jokes: it's about being funny in how you say things. Practise the skills you've learnt in chapter 20 on being funnier.

Conclude memorably

Conclude with a memorable, attention-grabbing sentence or story. Then thank the audience before you finish.

Keep it short but appropriate

There's usually lots happening on special occasions, so, often, the shorter the speech the better. At the same time, you've been asked to speak, so you need to make sure you follow through and do all that has been asked of you. The rule of thumb is to speak as long as you need to in order to do what you've been asked to do, but not much longer.

Business-life applications

Chapter 28
Business interviews

During job interviews, when they ask: 'What is your worst quality?' I always say: 'Flatulence.' That way, I get my own office.

DAN THOMPSON

At the end of 2011, I did a special one-day seminar for people who were out of work. I got a chance to talk to the participants about their biggest challenges and frustrations in searching for a job. Having also worked with recruitment companies and human-resource professionals, I've gained a unique insight into the most important aspects of the business-interview process.

Because of the economic recession, more people than ever have found themselves out of work. Being charismatic in interviews is all about making an impact. It's about understanding how the interviewer wants their potential candidate to come across.

You need to stand out when you're interviewed. Since you may well face a lot of competition, the more you can appear to be different from everyone else, the more likely the employer will be to remember you. Of course, the attitude, actions and abilities you possess will make a significant impact on your chances of success.

Another factor to bear in mind when applying for a job is your correspondence with the employer before the interview. It's also important to ensure that the cv you send is nicely laid out—clear, easy to read and of an appropriate length. They will be forming an impression of you from the moment they read about you, so the key is to make sure all your communication gives them the same message: I am right for the job.

ATTITUDE

To give yourself the best possible chance of getting the job you want, it's a good idea to have the most useful attitude when you go into the interview.

It's important to want this job but to remember that you don't need it. You might feel like you need a job, but not necessarily this one. This ensures that you avoid getting too nervous beforehand.

It's also important to remind yourself that you deserve this job, that you're the best candidate. If they knew how good you would be at this job, they'd hire you. That attitude will ensure that your frame of mind is one of confidence when you most need it.

There are plenty of other jobs that would suit you just as well as this one, but in this interview you're giving this employer an opportunity to get you. You're a great asset, and if you perform at your best in the interview you will give them some idea of this. If they say no they're simply making a mistake. The interview is to help them avoid making that mistake.

ACTIONS

Once you're in the right frame of mind and feeling what you need to be feeling, there are a number of actions you must take in order to be at your most effective and charismatic.

Make sure that you're smiling a **confident smile**, as if you're happy to meet the interviewers and are confident that they have met the right person for the job.

Use a firm—but not too firm—handshake.

Look the interviewer in the eye when you say hello, when they're speaking to you and most of the time when you're speaking. If there are a few interviewers, make sure you keep a consistent amount of eye contact with each of them.

Look impeccable, appropriate and as well as you possibly can. Spare no expense to make sure you look like someone they would want to hire.

Listen for the words they use and use the same words in return.

Build rapport with the interviewer using the suggestions given in chapter 14.

ABILITIES

Prepare ... prepare ... prepare

Make sure that before you go into any interview you've prepared the following:

Knowledge about yourself: Be aware of your strengths and weaknesses and how they relate to the job in question.

Knowledge about them: Know as much as you can about the kind of job you're going for and the type of employer that's hiring you. Ask specific questions to indicate that you've done your research.

Rehearse ... rehearse ... rehearse

It's good to rehearse different answers to questions you might be asked.

If you're asked for your weak points, make them seem like weaknesses but subtly also mention one of your strengths. For example: 'Well, sometimes I have become too involved in the job, but I've learnt recently to take a step back when I need to.' Try and nest every bad point inside two good ones.

Be specific and give specific examples. Many interviewers are used to hearing formulaic answers, so when you give clear, specific examples from your experience it will set you apart.

Remember to answer the questions asked. Often people will drift off to a prepared script, which can annoy interviewers. Make your answers fit the question neatly.

Always have a question to ask that focuses on the opportunities and what the best parts of the job are, rather than on the pension scheme and the money. You can ask those questions at a later stage.

Presentation

There are a few keys to presenting at interviews brilliantly.

Get yourself into a confident and relaxed state using some of the skills you've learnt in this book. The 'charisma squared' technique (chapter 10) is perfect for this. The trick is to build states of confidence and relaxation that you can anchor and trigger when you walk into the interview.

Avoid arrogance and cockiness, but act as though you expect the job. Answer the questions in a way that presupposes that you're the right person for it. For example, instead of saying, 'I feel that this job would challenge me . . .' you can say, 'I feel that this job *will* challenge me . . .'

Take a little time before answering and think through each question. Speak at an even pace and remember to concentrate on why you know you would be great for the job.

Be aware of your body language and act as confidently as possible.

Lastly, remember that the interview is not the be all and end all of your life. My crucial saying fits in perfectly here: 'If you want to get what you want, you need to let go of needing it.' When you let go of needing the interview, so that it doesn't matter as much, you can go into it with less desperation and more expectation—and that will help you maximise your chances of succeeding.

Chapter 29
Networking

The successful networkers I know, the ones receiving tonnes of referrals and feeling truly happy about themselves, continually put the other person's needs ahead of their own.

BOB BURG

I used to hate networking. You see, for a while I convinced myself that networking was all about rubbish small talk; you'd ask people boring questions about the most boring parts of their boring lives and they'd reciprocate and ask me the same. I'm not a fan of small talk. I like to get to know people really quickly. It's a skill I've learnt from travelling to so many places. When you don't have time you have to find other ways to make deep connections.

Over the course of the last few years, however, I've had my epiphany about networking. What I've discovered, having talked to a number of my friends who are really great networkers, is that they see it very differently, and when you look at it as they do it makes a big difference.

Instead of dreading networking, I now have a different set of beliefs about it, and I do it in my own way. Usually that involves getting to know people a lot quicker than you would normally, but that works for me. When you think about it differently, you realise that it's a great way of making a difference to more people, as well as of helping yourself in the process.

Networking is an art form. This art is all about presenting yourself in the most effective way to others in a corporate context. Others must see you in a way that will make them like and respect you at the same time. However, the politics of any company is also a huge factor and can often complicate matters. Effective networking involves certain attitudes, actions and abilities.

ATTITUDE

It's a good idea to keep the following in mind as you network:

The next meeting could be the one to radically change your life. You never know how important someone might turn out to be. So every person should be seen as a VIP. It's not always about who they are but about who they know.

There's always something you can like about everyone you meet. Focus on that. Business is not about being nice, but being nice can help you build relationships—and business is all about relationships.

It's not important to know everything about something: it's important to know something about everything. The world is full of opportunities for meeting someone who can really help you. The more you know, the more connections you'll be able to make.

Most people in business have their own agenda. They aren't opposed to yours, but theirs will always come first. Be careful who you trust and how much you trust them. Help others to get what they want and you can often get their help in return to get what you want.

ACTIONS

Always **look smart** and dress well and appropriately. Make sure your suit fits and that you present yourself well visually.

Develop a **resonant tone of voice**. This will improve how well other people hear you in meetings and presentations.

Always remember to **smile brightly**. A smile immediately makes you more attractive. Furthermore, it makes you look more approachable and like a nicer person. I know it's common sense, but in business most of us spend our days wading through life with scowls on our faces without even realising it. Smile!

Be clear about what you want from the interaction and **what you have to offer**.

Initiate the interaction and always ask what you can help them with first.

After the meeting make sure you **follow up** with an email and do your best to help them in any way you can. Enthuse about meeting them and lock in contact for the future.

ABILITIES
Remember names
Again, this is simple stuff, but why do we forget names? Is it that you 'just aren't any good' at remembering them? *No!* Most of the time it's because we never even hear the other person's name: we're too busy inside our head talking to ourselves about something stupid. When you meet someone, stop, listen to their name and, as you look at them, repeat it twice inside your head firmly and once or twice out loud in conversation. It'll help a lot.

Match up
Something useful to remember is that people like people who are like themselves. So, to create better relationships with people, breathe at the same rate as them, talk at the same rate, match their posture and so on. Unconsciously, this will send a signal of similarity to them and will improve the rapport between you.

Focus on the other person
Take the opportunity to make the other person feel good about themselves. Listen out for anything they seem proud of and send an indirect compliment their way. Understate the compliment so that it doesn't seem as if you're trying to gets something back from them, and make sure you truly believe it. People like people who make them feel good.

Key words
Listen out for key words and phrases the other person likes to use and repeat them to them. Be careful, though: don't overdo it. Use these words occasionally to keep them thinking that you're thinking like them.

Conversational positioning
Be aware strategically of how you're positioning yourself in every conversation and story you tell. Obviously, you need to ensure that you don't go over the top and name-drop excessively, but it's an important skill to practise getting your point across by means of what you drop into the conversation effortlessly.

Avoid confrontation

It's important to stay on everyone's good side as far as possible. While remaining true to yourself, avoid making enemies or getting into big disagreements. The fewer people out to get you, the easier your job will be. You can 'see where they're coming from' without directly agreeing.

Chapter 30
Sales

You can have everything in life you want, if you will just help other people get what they want.

ZIG ZIGLAR

A few years ago, I had two people from the aid agency Concern call to my door. As I listened to them, I noticed that they were using a number of influence skills to 'sell' me on the charity. My 'nerd' brain took over and I started to ask myself what else they could be using. So I invited them in and signed up. (I believe in Concern as a fantastic organisation.) I then proceeded to deconstruct what they were using, and I started giving them suggestions for how they could improve. Half an hour later, they bounced out with another donation and pages of notes on what else they could do to become even more persuasive.

The very best salespeople are often charismatic when they sell. The reason is simple: charisma is an incredibly useful skill to have when trying to influence or convince others. The art of sales is about using the skills of influence and persuasion to sell whatever products or services you're selling. You do this by creating the right feelings in the other person and leading them to share your vision.

Sales is full of tactics and techniques that work on the other person at a psychological and emotional level. Perhaps your greatest resource, however, is the relationship you create with the other person. This stems from your ability to make a powerful impression in their mind and to get them to want to connect with you more. We live in an age when much of the market involves relationships and strategic selling. That means we can no longer rely on smart tricks to get a share of the market. We must make the customer enjoy doing business with us.

There are a number of critical attitudes, actions and abilities that will help you to become a much more effective and charismatic salesperson.

ATTITUDE

To become successful in sales, there are a number of different ideas to keep in mind.

Rejection simply means you need to make another phone call or knock on another door. It's something to learn from and immediately move on from to the next customer.

What you're selling is going to make the customer's life better and is well worth the investment. You have to first remind yourself of the value you offer to your clients in order to be able to get them to see it.

You have the potential to be great at what you do, and you can learn how to become even better than you could have imagined. You have to first remind yourself of the value of yourself or the product before connecting with your clients. You have the chance to make a really positive difference to their life.

If they say no, they simply haven't got it yet. Every no you hear must not be taken as a pure rejection. All it means is that you haven't yet found the best way to explain it to the other person.

There are millions of people who want this. You just have to find them. Scarcity can frighten you, but it's a silly thought. The reality is that there are many people who would love and value your product. Often the key is just to find them.

ACTIONS

Charismatic salespeople tend to do a number of things that help the customer to feel connected with them.

Smile brightly and genuinely. Make the other person feel like you're glad you're talking with them.

Listen. Pay attention to exactly what they say and learn what you can about their goals, aspirations, values and beliefs.

Read them. Learn what you can about their background and pay attention to any non-verbal information that comes your way, so that you can understand them better. Their clothes, shoes and body language will all teach you valuable information about them.

Talk in terms of their interests. That's what they care about.

Make them feel important. This is about them, not you. Ask them questions about themselves and focus on giving them a really wonderful customer-service experience. You're not just in 'sales' but in 'customer relations'.

Build rapport by matching and mirroring them. This is a

powerful way to create an instant connection with them. To ensure that the connection is as strong as possible ask yourself the question, 'What do you genuinely like about the client?' This will put you in exactly the right frame of mind for communicating with them.

Dress appropriately. Wear what you think the other person wants to see. If you think they'd prefer you to dress in such a way that they feel comfortable talking to you, you can look more relaxed. Often they will prefer if you're dressed in an extremely professional manner, as it will seem aspirational from their point of view. They will buy a very expensive watch from a sales agent wearing a very expensive suit; they will buy an expensive bag from a shop-owner who dresses to impress.

ABILITIES
There are a number of skills to practise to ensure that you boost your sales.

Remember to get them saying 'Yes, yes, yes.' Ask a series of questions you know they'll answer yes to. This will develop a subconscious sense that they agree with you.

Remember people's names. When you do, it's a good start. When you don't, it's a terrible start.

Use as many **sensory channels** as possible to describe the products and services and their benefits.

Use the seven pillars of persuasion, as described in chapter 19. Come across as confident, expert, likeable, similar, engaging, trustworthy and open when you're communicating with them.

Use language in the most useful ways to persuade the person of the value of the product you're selling. Use lots of **truisms followed by presuppositions** (see chapter 19). You build credibility and then you use those structures.

Chapter 31
Leadership

Captain America: Sergeant! I want you to station your men in all these buildings, and I need a perimeter all the way down to 39th.

Police sergeant: Why should I take orders from you?

[Five extra-terrestrial life forms with special lasers arrive, and Captain America kills them all one by one.]

Police Sergeant [on radio]: *I want men posted in all these buildings! And I want a perimeter all the way down to 39th!*

'THE AVENGERS'

I peeked through my fingers as the greatest soccer player in the world, Lionel Messi, attacked again. It was Parkhead, Glasgow. The date was 7 November 2012. It was the 125th anniversary of the Glasgow Celtic Football Club and they were facing the sublime Barcelona in the European Champions League. Celtic were supposed to have no chance whatsoever. However, they were in an incredible position. Having had 11 per cent of the possession, they managed to score twice and were leading Barcelona with seconds to go, two goals to one. There were 60,000 of us on our feet willing the referee to blow the whistle. And then, a miracle happened. The match ended.

How did such an event happen? Of course there were the wonderful warriors of Glasgow Celtic, the players who delivered some of the best performances of their careers. But perhaps one of the biggest factors was the manager of the team, Neil Lennon. A natural leader, he proved himself over his years with Celtic as a captain and then a manager. On this damp and cool night, Neil created the winning strategy and inspired his entire team towards digging deep within themselves for greatness. And afterwards, he heaped praise on the players themselves, focusing on their brilliance rather than on his own. A shining example of a truly great leader.

Neil's passion has on occasion got him into trouble, but it has also made him even more popular with the fans. People want to know that you believe in the same cause as they do. They want to know that you share their pain and that you want success as much as they do, if not more so. When Neil talks in a post-match interview he does so bluntly and honestly. He is straightforward and calls things as he sees them. He takes responsibility for what goes wrong and believes in the talent of his team. He knows how to get through to them and how to do so in order to bring out their best. He has the ability to learn from his mistakes and also has his own mentors, including the chief shareholder of Celtic, Dermot Desmond, who regularly advises him. Desmond, himself a hugely successful Irish businessman and lifelong Celtic supporter, is a fantastic role model for leadership.

A leader is someone who inspires, influences and ignites the potential of their team. They understand how to communicate individually and in groups and deliver their message in a compelling way. They transmit trust, belief and passion to those who work for them. They create entire movements because of their grand visions and deep-seated belief in the potential greatness of those they work with. In many ways the art of leadership is about cultivating respect from your fellow-workers, peers and members of staff. It's about demonstrating the strength of character and skill that justifies positioning yourself as someone to be listened to and valued.

A word that's often linked with leadership is 'charisma'. When a leader is charismatic, they stand out more. They're far more compelling in how they put their point across, and they tend to build a far greater sense of loyalty from their team. To understand how you can apply what you've learnt to becoming a more effective leader, let's examine the attitudes, actions and abilities of the most charismatic leaders.

ATTITUDE

As a charismatic leader, you need to know the importance of thinking differently.

You need to remember that you have what it takes to get the best out of your team. You must realise that you can inspire, motivate and unleash the power of your team by leading them successfully. The reality is that you can inspire people easily and motivate them effectively. The skills to inspire, energise and motivate lie in your ability to communicate charismatically, which you've learnt in this book.

You must be prepared to do whatever it is you ask of those who follow you. By leading by example you will find it far easier to establish credibility and loyalty in your team. You can lead your team through any and every challenge in a way that helps you all develop more wonderfully. Of course, it's vital to believe in them and their ability to triumph in order for them to believe in themselves.

It's also important to have a clear vision of where you're all going and to have an action plan for how you can get there. You need to be very clear about what your vision is and be able to clearly and precisely present that vision to your team. Every member of the team is a vital member, and you need to work collectively towards the achievement of your goals and the betterment of yourselves. It's a good idea to see all your team as being necessary for, and fundamental to, your overall success. By doing so, you help transmit that message to them, thereby emphasising the power of teamwork.

ACTIONS

Charismatic leaders tend to do a number of things that build a loyal support and following. Here are some suggestions for acting like a charismatic leader:

Articulate your vision clearly for your followers. Max Weber, one of the most popular theorists to discuss charisma, argued that vision is one of the most important characteristics of a charismatic leader.

Make sure you look like a leader. Always dress more stylishly and impressively than those you work with, even when dressing casually. Dress like them but better than them. Everything about you has to say 'leader'.

When you talk to someone, make sure you **listen well to what they're saying** and communicate to them as if they were the most important person to you at that time.

Move through the world **looking confident and in control**. Smile a certain smile that suggests that you're very sure you're going to get your way today, but avoid giving an impression of arrogance. Keep your expressions positive and reassuring, regardless of how you may feel inside.

Learn to **master rapport** with all sorts of people.

Take the initiative and begin to put plans in operation that will help get you and your team to where you all need to be.

Develop people by learning how to **give feedback usefully**. Learn how to make people feel valued and inspired by being inspired and motivated yourself, and learn how to create positive states in others.

ABILITIES

The very best leaders understand that they need to refine a number of skills to be at their best.

Become more **self-aware** and know your strengths and weaknesses. Be open to feedback from others and learn as much as you can.

Clarify what is expected, what is desired and what is required and determine how to get there.

Develop your skills of **public speaking** so you can inspire your entire team at once.

Find interesting ways to get across your point. Since **stories** are far more memorable than statements, practise using stories that get people thinking.

Learn how to master **influencing** other people and practise doing so to assist your team in working in the most productive and effective way.

Build good **credibility** by demonstrating that you understand the difficulties and challenges faced by your team.

Chapter 32
Business presentations

They may forget what you said, but they will never forget how you made them feel.

CARL W. BUECHNER

When I'm asked to do a business presentation, the stakes are usually high. If I do a great one, I get hired. If not, I won't. That's the kind of pressure I face. Most presentations haven't got as much riding on them. Unfortunately, that can make things quite boring. Often it's a case of listening to someone droning on about something you don't care about, giving you information you don't need to know, in a way that makes you ask yourself whether anyone in the room would notice if you went for a snooze.

I once witnessed a speaker present for forty minutes on how to do interesting presentations. The problem was that he was agony to listen to as he read monotonously from his notes, standing behind a podium. I wanted to scream, but I was too sleepy!

The ability some people have to make an audience miserable for an hour never ceases to amaze me. And the saddest thing is that you can become massively more interesting and influential by following a few simple rules and guiding principles.

Making presentations to a business audience is a perfect opportunity to stand out as a charismatic communicator. The art of successful business presenting and training is about conveying key ideas, skills and knowledge in a way that people like, understand and remember. It's about understanding the importance of influencing a group's state while you're talking to them. If you pay attention to how your audience feels and how you want them to feel, you will have a big advantage in the corporate arena. So, what are the most useful attitudes, actions and abilities to have?

ATTITUDE

There are a number of ideas to keep in mind when you're presenting or training in a corporate context.

Firstly, the audience are probably already bored. It's your job to give them something of interest or something entertaining to listen to or learn from. What you have to say is of great value to them. They're listening to you for a reason: it's important for them to hear what you have to say. Entertainment is usually a bonus. Most people don't expect to be entertained when someone speaks to them. They learnt at an early age that when someone comes to speak to them, they're forced to listen. So, you've got absolutely nothing to lose.

Also, remember that you're in control of the audience. You can make them stand, sit or touch their toes, and you can make them smile—all by telling them to do so. If you don't get the responses you want, you need to change what you're doing. Focus on changing their state. The state of your audience is extremely important if they're to learn well. You must get your audience in the right emotional state and frame of mind for them to learn in the best way.

Now, they may not always reveal what they feel. Remember that, even when they look serious or are frowning, your audience will often be smiling inside. In groups, people get trapped in a group mask in which they don't want to stand out, so they keep still as much as possible.

You're only ever talking to one person at a time. Remember to breathe deeply and pause before you begin. Scan the room and fix your eyes for a few seconds on some individuals. Remember, they're human.

ACTIONS

The next thing is to do what's necessary to grab and keep their attention.

On stage, **look as well as you can** but also look appropriate for the occasion.

Use modern technology, especially for short presentations. Video is a smart move.

Train your voice so that it's resonant and sounds authoritative.

Stand with one foot in front of the other. This ensures that you have solid balance and that you can turn and have depth in front of an audience.

Move about on stage when appropriate.

Make everything more animated when you're on stage. Use hand gestures and facial expressions a little bit more than normal, but do so naturally.

As soon as you get on stage **smile and look as many of the audience members in the eye as you can.** When you say hello and introduce yourself, say it with as much personal warmth as possible.

ABILITIES

In addition to the skills described in the chapter on public speaking (chapter 27), here are some suggestions for business presentations.

Preparation

Whenever you're preparing a presentation keep the following questions in mind:

What do I want to accomplish with this presentation?

What research do I need to have done on the subject?

Who can help me?

How will I introduce the subject?

How will I make my points?

How will I conclude the talk?

How will I make the presentation easy to understand for the audience?

How will I make the presentation fascinating to the audience and keep their attention?

How can I break the ice in the group?

How can I use my voice in the most effective way?

How will I stand, sit, move and look on stage?

Delivery

Pay attention to the audience

Always ask yourself, 'How can I get and keep their interest and attention?' Notice when your audience is getting tired or seems bored, and change what you're doing.

Use quotations

When you quote someone it enables you to put across a point in a powerful and succinct way. It can also give the point more authority.

Use ice-breakers

When giving presentations it's often good to stop talking after a few minutes and do an exercise in which your audience can start to meet each other. Usually people will feel a little apprehensive about presentations, as they're uncertain about what to expect. When you get them to meet each other and have fun through exercises it enables them to feel more at ease.

Use clever arguments and logic

Make a statement and then back it up. Logic works by making statements and supporting them with evidence.

Overcome potential objections

You can overcome potential objections by being the first to mention them. Bring them up ahead of time and inoculate the audience against them. You can do this by working out what objections or problems an audience might have and then talking about these problems. You can then put the problem into the past and also identify it as a thought rather than as a fact.

Next, say the problem or objection in an annoying tone of voice. This attaches it to a negative feeling, and people will unconsciously want to associate with it less. Then use the word 'but', which immediately cancels the impact of the rebuttal and focuses (positively) on what you're about to say next. Finally, use a presupposition and state a new way of thinking about the problem, or use an answer to it directly after the presupposition. For example: 'Now, some people have thought [objection or problem], but most people realise that [answer to objection or problem].'

Conclude memorably

Conclude with a memorable, attention-grabbing sentence or story while summarising your presentation simply.

Chapter 33

Conclusion: The charismatic communicator

I don't have delusions of grandeur. I have an actual recipe for grandeur.

EDDIE MORRA

Congratulations on getting to the final chapter of this book. Many people buy a book and then fail to read past the first chapter. Life gets in the way and they find themselves focusing on something else. However, if there's one quality I've noticed in the most successful people I've met it's that they are obsessive learners and read a lot. It's one of the biggest contributing factors to them seeming to have the 'edge' over everyone else. Having found yourself here, you now see the road diverging in front of you.

One of those roads is the one that most people have been down and that most people will go down in the future. It is the road of doing the same things in the same way and living the same life as always. 'After all,' these people say to themselves, 'it's only a book. A book can't make that much of a difference.' This road is a very busy one, and you'll find plenty of traffic here. But it won't matter much, because this is a road that doesn't go anywhere anyway.

The other road is far quieter. Few people have been down it. It is a road filled with adventure, fun and challenge. It is a road that only the very best communicators in the world have travelled on. It is a road that only those committed to living an amazing life will follow. There is not much traffic. The world gets prettier the further you go down that road, and it leads to a destination of fulfilment and achievement.

It's up to you which road you go down. I hope you decide on the road of adventure. By implementing what you've learnt here, you will find yourself on this road of adventure. If you decide to do so it can truly enhance your life.

NEXT STEPS

Now that you're returning to your life, what are you going to do? Are you going to use the ideas, skills and suggestions in this book to live a more charismatic life? Only you can decide. There are so many things you can do and implement in all areas of your life. The question is, Will you implement them?

You see, the great news is that if you do you will discover that wonderful changes are in store for you. All those situations you avoided because you cared what other people thought will no longer be ones you want to avoid. Instead, you will move through the world with quiet confidence and self-assurance. You will believe more in yourself. You will do so because you think differently about yourself now and because you think differently about relating to others. You feel free of the enemies of charisma that limited you and kept you in the chains of fear and insecurity.

Living more charismatically is about moving through the world with a sense of confidence and security in yourself. It is about knowing the value of who you are and about being able to express yourself passionately to others. It is about revelling in the art of brilliant communication and enjoying all the success that the power of influence brings.

This book is a workbook designed to get you to make certain changes in the way you think, feel, behave and act. It is designed to help you fundamentally alter your relationship with yourself and with others. It is designed to get you to overcome the things that used to limit you, and to enable you to have the wonderful freedom that comes with being as charismatic as you truly are.

Once upon a time, you were born. You were born with great potential to be the best you could be. You were born into a world with a great many other people so that you could connect with them and enter their lives as they enter yours. This book is one way of beginning to enter more lives and of making your own life one in which you live wonderfully, freely and fully.

I hope that, when you eventually leave this world, you are able to look back at your life and be happy with all the connections you made, all the people you talked to, all the wonderful experiences you had, and say, 'I am fulfilled.' I hope this book can be something that contributes to this moment. This is a very simple book. It just needs to be used.

Imagine people hanging on your every word, looking at you with absolute fascination as you speak with confidence. Imagine the most attractive people you meet being interested in you for reasons they can't put their finger on and just wanting to be around you for reasons they don't know. Imagine being able to present brilliantly and get a crowded room laughing at every joke you tell.

Now, do it.

This book did not begin a year ago, when I began to collect my thoughts on the charismatic edge. It did not begin ten years ago, when I began my 'Art of Charisma' courses. This book began twenty years ago. It began not as an idea but as a question; not as a process but as a seed of hope; not as a lesson but as a burning desire.

The information you need to step forward, step up, stand out and stand for the best version of yourself is out there. My passion has been studying everything I could find in the area and testing it, applying it and using it.

So, in this book you can find everything distilled down to the essentials. You can see the thousands of hours of research that have gone into this, the tens of thousands of people who have been participants on courses I've delivered in more than twenty countries, the hundreds of books left dog-eared . . . All of them contributed to answering a question in two parts: Can anyone become charismatic? and, if so, how?

The pain I experienced back in my younger years of being unpopular, the frustration I experienced at being misunderstood, the loneliness I experienced at being different—all these ignited a burning desire that moved mountains and helped transform my world. Sometimes all it takes is a question or a seed of hope and a desire to do more, know more, learn more, feel more, be more. Because you *can* be more.

You don't *have* to be more. You are perfect just as you are. But you *can* be more. So, why not? Why not you? Why not now? For it is in the decision you make, right here and now, that lies the power to light a fire deep inside your soul. It is a flame that can pass from person to person, much like the Olympic torch. Like that torch, it can spread far and wide to everyone you come in contact with. Like that torch, it can symbolise the greatness of humankind. Like that torch, it can inspire the world.

I'm not sure what drew you to this book. Maybe you're going

through a rough patch. Maybe you're lonely. Maybe you're doing great but looking for an edge in your business. Maybe you want to become a better presenter. Whatever your reason for picking up this book, the answer lies in the same old message. It's a message I badly want you to get, because I know what will happen if you do: your world will be filled with magic.

The truth is that the words written here produce magic only when they are taken in and used. They produce magic only when you take heed of the incantations for freedom and joy that exist herein. They produce magic only when you value the importance of applying them to your world.

On my web site, www.charisma.ie, you'll find some free videos dedicated to helping you apply what you've been learning. There's an online course you can do (the Online Charisma Training Academy) and training I give if you want to go deeper. You see, this isn't about me writing a book: this is a mission. I have grand aims, grand ambitions, grand ideals. I want to impact your life, rock your world.

On all my journeys throughout the world, I've met thousands of individuals from every walk of life. I've met some who affected me deeply and some I can't recall. The difference was in who they were with me. The reality is that it always begins there. Your inner world. Your character. Your attitude. Your philosophy. Your psychology. Your perspective. That's where the journey begins.

LIVING CHARISMATICALLY EVER AFTER

It's about you realising that you were born with a natural gift called charisma. It's about understanding that you were supposed to be unique, yourself, fully you. It's about knowing that you were never supposed to be afraid of the rejections that are an inevitable part of life; that you were never supposed to be frightened of the failures you would encounter; and that you were never supposed to be fearful of looking foolish or silly, embarrassed or ridiculous, knowing that these experiences are natural, normal and not in any way a declaration of you. It's about discovering that you decide who you're going to be, that you define your character and the person you are. You have a choice to feel how you choose to feel. It's up to you. It's your time.

For it is only in getting to this place, accepting this great gift, that we can decide to carry the flame forward and out into the world. And we must do so with a spring in our step, light in our eyes and grace in our movements, because these movements too carry a message. They tell the world *how* we are, if not always *who* we are. It's crucial that we act on this planet as we want this planet to see us. To dress and talk, smile and walk, stand and speak with language, verbal and non-verbal, and tell others how to see us, how to hear us, how to feel about us.

And we make this flame brighter by learning the skills, the disciplines, the principles, the understandings known to only a small selection of the greatest communicators the world has ever seen. When we learn to do what they do we get the opportunity to make the kind of impact they made.

Finally, we must decide where we are going to bring this flame. Who are we going to inspire? Where are we going to apply what we've learnt? What are we going to do now?

My philosophy of life comes down to this: we are alive to impact the world and allow the world to impact us. Since we are on this planet together, it makes sense that we connect with each other as best we can. I learnt very early in life that in order for me to be happy, getting on with others was a necessary step. It doesn't mean you have to have everyone like you, nor does it mean you need to be around people all the time to be happy. Rather, it means that your ability to connect with and impact others is crucial for the quality of life you will have.

Being more charismatic helps you to step up so that you start to really like yourself. It helps you to step up so you can overcome the fears of failure, rejection and embarrassment that threaten to stifle your growth and potential. It helps you to step up to think in a new way about yourself, others and the whole process of communication.

Being more charismatic helps you to step forward and be counted by coming across in a more engaging way. It helps you to step forward and create a powerful first impression. It helps you to look and speak more effectively so that you impact others more.

Being more charismatic helps you to stand out from the crowd with skills of influence and persuasion. It helps you to stand out in the way you tell stories and make people laugh. It helps you to stand out and speak in public in a way that inspires and affects your audience memorably.

Being more charismatic helps you to stand for the best possible version of yourself. It helps you to stand for the qualities and skills that help you in business and in your personal life. It helps you stand for the attitudes that can give you the edge you need in interviews, dates, meetings, networking engagements—even in your social life.

There are so many wonderful ways in which charisma can improve the quality of your life, but none of this matters unless you follow it through. The world is full of stories of people who might have succeeded but didn't, who might have got that job but didn't, who might have won the heart of that person but didn't. It's easy to do nothing. It's easy to hold yourself back. It's easy to make excuses about why you aren't implementing the skills you've learnt here.

It's easy . . . but it's stupid. The book you hold in your hands contains some extremely valuable information. When I first sat down to write it my intention was to deliver something that could help a person transform their world. I believe that the right words said in the right way to the right person at the right time are magical.

So, as you put this book down, I ask you to take a moment and make a promise to yourself. The only thing we can be sure of is that one day we will move on from this world. When we do, the question we will ask ourselves is 'How did we live?' Make a promise that you will up your game, that you will step up and practise what you've learnt in these pages. You have this one life to go for it.

When I wanted to die all those years ago, I wanted to die so that I wouldn't be in pain any more. Now I want to make sure that, when I do go, I go with a smile on my face. A smile that says, in the words of the charismatic Frank Sinatra, 'I lived a life that's full.' My journey is continuing, and I'm blessed to have connected with you on that journey too. I hope you do apply what you learnt and that, in some way, I helped you make a difference to your life, your world.

I promised myself a long time ago that I would face the dark feelings and move through them, that I would face the challenges and handle them, that I would face the setbacks and bounce back with every fibre of my being. For you can be sure that some bumps in the road lie ahead; but if you dig deep, if you reach within and if you step up, you'll find that your character will emerge. The real you. The very best you. The you that you were always supposed to be.

In that moment, you'll be able to handle anything. You'll be able to conquer anything. You'll be able to triumph over anything. Adversity will not stop you: it will simply help you grow. Obstacles and problems will educate you, and you'll continue to move forward. As humans, we have been born with the ability to do incredible things. Most of all we have been born with a spirit that can lead us towards the brightest future we can possibly imagine.

This is your time to shine. This is your time to design the kind of life you were born to live. C'mon. You can do it. No more living a limited life. Applying the secrets shared in this book can enable you to live a life so much better than the one you've lived until now. And remember: you can be more . . . because you are.

Recommended reading

Atkinson, Max, *Lend Me Your Ears: All You Need to Know about Making Speeches and Presentations*, New York: Oxford University Press, 2005.

Bandler, Richard, *Get the Life You Want*, New York: Harper Collins, 2008.

Bandler, Richard, *Richard Bandler's Guide to Trance-formation: How to Harness the Power of Hypnosis to Ignite Effortless and Lasting Change*, New York: Harper Collins, 2008.

Bandler, Richard, *Using Your Brain for a Change*, Boulder (Colo): Real People Press, 1985.

Bandler, Richard, and Fitzpatrick, Owen, *Conversations with Richard Bandler*, Deerfield Beach (Fla): Health Communications, 2005.

Bandler, Richard, and Fitzpatrick, Owen, *Memories* (in press).

Bandler, Richard, and Grinder, John, *Frogs into Princes: Neuro Linguistic Programming*, Boulder (Colo): Real People Press, 1979.

Bandler, Richard, and LaValle, John, *Persuasion Engineering*, Capitola (Calif.): Meta Publications, 1996.

Bandler, Richard, Roberti, Alessio, and Fitzpatrick, Owen, *The Ultimate Introduction to NLP*, New York: Harper Collins (2013).

Carnegie, Dale, *How to Win Friends and Influence People*, New York: Simon and Schuster, 1936.

Cialdini, Robert B., *Influence: The Psychology of Persuasion* (Collins Business Essentials), New York: William Morrow, 1993.

Colbert, Brian, *From Ordinary to Extraordinary*, Dublin: Gill & Macmillan, 2013.

Colbert, Brian, *The Happiness Habit: Choose the Path to a Better Life*, Dublin: Newleaf, 2010.

Covey, Stephen R., *The 7 Habits of Highly Effective People*, New York: Free Press, 2004.

Duhigg, Charles, *The Power of Habit: Why We Do What We Do in Life and Business*, New York: Random House, 2011.

Fitzpatrick, Owen, *Not Enough Hours*, Dublin: Poolbeg, 2009.

Fox Cabane, Olivia, *The Charisma Myth: How Anyone Can Master the Art and Science of Personal Magnetism*, New York: Portfolio Penguin, 2012.

Gottman, John M., and Silver, Nan, *The Seven Principles for Making Marriage Work: A Practical Guide from the Country's Foremost Relationship Expert*, New York: Three Rivers Press, 2000.

Kahneman, Daniel, *Thinking Fast and Slow*, New York: Farrar, Straus and Giroux, 2011.

Robbins, Anthony, *Awaken the Giant Within: How to Take Immediate Control of Your Mental, Emotional, Physical and Financial Destiny!* New York: Free Press, 1992.

Wiseman, Richard, *Rip It Up: The Radically New Approach to Changing Your Life*, London: Macmillan, 2012.

Bibliography

Abrecht, Karl, *Social Intelligence: The New Science of Success, Economies, Societies and Nations*, San Francisco: Pfeiffer, 2005.

Bandler, Richard, *Time for a Change*, Capitola (Calif.): Meta Publications, 1993.

Benton, D. A., *Executive Charisma: Six Steps to Mastering the Art of Leadership*, New York: McGraw-Hill, 2005.

Berry, Mary Frances, Gottheimer, Josh, and Sorenson, Theodore C., *Power in Words: The Stories behind Barack Obama's Speeches, from the State House to the White House*, Boston (Mass.): Beacon Press, 2010.

Cohen, Steve, *Win the Crowd: Unlock the Secrets of Influence, Charisma and Showmanship*, New York: Harper Collins, 2005.

Cron, Lisa, *Wired for Story: The Writer's Guide to Using Brain Science to Hook Readers from the Very First Sentence*, Berkeley (Calif.): Ten Speed Press, 2012.

Denning, Stephen, *The Secret Language of Leadership: How Leaders Inspire Action through Narrative*, San Francisco: Jossey-Bass, 2007.

DiSalvo, Danny, *What Makes Your Brain Happy and Why You Should Do the Opposite*, Amherst (NY): Prometheus Books, 2011.

Driver, Janine, *You Say More Than You Think: A 7-Day Plan for Using the New Body Language to Get What You Want*, New York: Three Rivers Press, 2011.

Ellsberg, Michael, *Power of Eye Contact: Your Secret for Success in Business, Love and Life*, New York: William Morrow Paperbacks, 2010.

Gallo, Carime, *The Presentation Secrets of Steve Jobs: How to Be Insanely Great in Front of Any Audience*, New York: McGraw-Hill Professional, 2009.

Goleman, Daniel, *Emotional Intelligence: Why It Can Matter More Than IQ*, New York: Bantam Books, 2006.

Goleman, Daniel, *Social Intelligence: The New Science of Human Relationships*, New York: Bantam Books, 2006.

Gottschall, Jonathan, *The Storytelling Animal: How Stories Make Us Human*, New York: Houghton Mifflin Harcourt, 2012.

Hansen, Drew, *The Dream: Martin Luther King, Jr, and the Speech that Inspired a Nation*, New York: Harper Collins, 2005.

Johnston, Christopher, *Microstyle: The Art of Writing Little*, New York: Norton, 2011.

Jones, Clarence B., and Connelly, Stuart, *Behind the Dream: The Making of the Speech That Transformed a Nation*, Basingstoke (Hants): Palgrave Macmillan, 2012.

Kinsey Goman, Carol, *The Nonverbal Advantage: Secrets and Science of Body Language at Work*, San Francisco: Berrett-Koehler, 2008.

Kinsey Goman, Carol, *The Silent Language of Leadership: How Body Language Can Help—or Hurt—How You Lead*, San Francisco: Jossey-Bass, 2011.

Klein, Woody, *All the Presidents' Spokesmen: Spinning the News: White House Press Secretaries from Franklin D. Roosevelt to George W. Bush*, Westport (Conn.): Greenwood, 2008.

Kotter, John P., *Buy In: Saving Your Good Idea from Getting Shot Down*, Boston (Mass.): Harvard Business Review Press, 2010.

McCann, Deiric, Haney, Bud, and Sirbasku, Jim, *Leadership Charisma*, Conway (Ark.): s and н Publishing, 2011.

McKenna, Paul, *Change Your Life in Seven Days*, New York: Bantam Press, 2005.

Murray, Kevin, *The Language of Leaders: How Top CEOs Communicate to Inspire, Influence, and Achieve Results*, London: Kogan Page, 2012.

Navarro, Joe, and Karlins, Marvin, *What Every Body is Saying: An Ex-FBI Agent's Guide to Speed-Reading People*, New York: William Morrow Paperbacks, 2008.

Perloff, Richard M., *The Dynamics of Persuasion: Communication and Attitudes in the Twenty-First Century*, New York: Taylor and Francis, 2012.

Phillips, Donald T., *The Clinton Charisma: A Legacy of Leadership*, Basingstoke (Hants): Palgrave Macmillan, 2007.

Rees, Laurence, *The Dark Charisma of Adolf Hitler: Leading Millions into the Abyss*, London: Ebury Press, 2012.

Sibenius, James, *3D Negotiation: Powerful Tools to Change the Game in Your Most Important Deals*, Boston (Mass.): Harvard Business Review Press, 2006.

Spence, Gerry, *Win Your Case: How to Present, Persuade, and Prevail—Every Place, Every Time*, New York: St Martin's Press, 2005.

Steel, Jon, *Perfect Pitch: The Art of Selling Ideas and Winning New Business*, New York: Wiley, 2006.

Sunstein, Cass R., and Thaler, Richard H., *Nudge: Improving Decisions about Health, Wealth, and Happiness*, New Haven (Conn.): Yale University Press, 2008.

RECOMMENDED WEBSITES
www.owenfitzpatrick.com
www.nlp.ie
www.charisma.ie
www.facebook.com/ofi23
www.twitter.com/owenfitzp
www.charismatrainingacademy.com
www.briancolbert.ie
www.richardbandler.com
www.purenlp.com
www.hiddendepth.ie
www.maxatkinson.blogspot.jp
www.voicecoach.ie
www.meta-nlp.co.uk
www.nlpitaly.com
www.linguisticintelligence.org
www.ziglar.com
www.joelroberts.com
www.digipill.com
www.theultimateintroductiontonlp.com

CHARISMA TRAINING ACADEMY
This online course is packed full of videos on every aspect of charisma. It includes some of the footage from the two Charisma Bootcamps and some focused online tutorials on different elements of charisma.

If you become a member, you will have lifetime access to a library of videos, MP3 files and PDFs that share with you the keys to becoming more charismatic. For more information go to www.charismatraining academy.com or check out the other websites, www.owenfitzpatrick.com and www.charisma.ie.

THE IRISH INSTITUTE OF NLP

Brian Colbert and Owen Fitzpatrick jointly founded the Irish Institute of NLP (neuro-linguistic programming) in 2001. There are only two NLP master trainers in Ireland. Owen and Brian are highly recommended by Richard Bandler (joint founder of NLP) and the Society of NLP, the largest and oldest NLP training body in the world. They're known for their remarkable ability to work together seamlessly and with great humour. Their unique training style reveals their great friendship and synergy.

Since they founded the institute, they have presented NLP seminars and training in Europe, Asia and the Americas. They provide regular licensed NLP practitioners, NLP business practitioners, NLP master practitioners and NLP coaching certification programmes and also offer various evening workshops and life-enhancement weekends.

Owen and Brian both have publications in print. Brian has authored the best-selling book *The Happiness Habit*. He is well known for his appearances on national television and radio and in print media. Owen is known for his popular RTÉ television series 'Not Enough Hours'. Brian and Owen also offer corporate consulting and present in-house training to the corporate sector in the areas of communication, sales, motivation, stress management, creativity and the business applications of NLP. To learn NLP in Ireland, or to make your life and business better, visit the institute's website today.

Irish Institute of NLP
84 Sundrive Road
Kimmage
Dublin 12

Telephone: +353 (0)1 490 2923
Email: theresa@nlp.ie

Websites:
www.nlp.ie
www.briancolbert.ie
www.owenfitzpatrick.com